THE DIARIES OF THREE SURGEONS OF PATNA 1763

THE DIARIES OF THREE SURGEONS OF PATNA 1763

Edited By

WALTER K. FIRMINGER

GYAN

Published by

GYAN

Gyan Publishing House
5, Ansari Road
Daryaganj, New Delhi-110002
Phone: 011-47034999, 9811692060
E-mail: books@gyanbooks.com

Distribution Network
gyanbooks.com
India, USA, Canada, UK, Australia, France

ISBN : 978-81-212-9838-4 (PB)
First Published, 1909

2nd Impression 2023

Printed at: Gyan Press, Delhi.

THE DIARIES OF THREE SURGEONS OF PATNA 1763
Edited by: WALTER K. FIRMINGER

THE DIARIES OF THREE SURGEONS OF PATNA

1763.

EDITED BY WALTER K. FIRMINGER.

1909

PREFACE.

NEARLY fifty years ago, MR. TALBOYS WHEELER called attention to the existence of these Diaries, and in 1878 he gave a few very meagre extracts from them in his *Early Records of British India*. Last year, guided by MR. TALBOYS WHEELER's *Report*, the old papers were searched out for me by the kind officials of the Imperial Record Department, and the Government of India most graciously accorded me permission to copy and publish them. It was only after the printing had been done, that I discovered that MR. H. BEVERIDGE had published Anderson's Diary in the *Calcutta Review* of October 1884, and Campbell's Diary and Fullarton's Relation in a subsequent number. But if, in view of this fact, the present publication loses the charm of novelty, I cannot but think it will be extremely useful. For, in the first place, back numbers of the *Calcutta Review* are not very easily procured; and, in the second, when I compared my printed text with that of MR. BEVERIDGE, I found that the document I was working at was a far better copy of the original than the one which MR. BEVERIDGE found among the Hastings' papers at the British Museum. Although the parallel columns I have made use of are not beautiful—and they have necessitated the use of small type,—it will be an advantage to the student to have the events of each day clearly before his eyes. Fullarton gives us a "Naration" not a "Diary": but I have thought it best to break up his paragraphs and to space them according to date.

MR. BEVERIDGE in his reproduction of the Diaries did not follow the writers' spelling of place and personal names; but, with all deference to so eminent a scholar, I have not followed MR. BEVERIDGE's example in this respect.

WALTER K. FIRMINGER.

SHILLONG, ASSAM, *July 23rd, 1909.*

P. S.—I have preferred "Fullarton" to "Fullerton," but I am not sure that I am correct.

INTRODUCTION.

"Nothing in history or fiction, not even the story which Ugolino told in the sea of everlasting ice, after he had wiped his bloody lips on the scalp of his murderer, approaches the horrors which were recounted by the few survivors of that night." So Lord Macaulay wrote of the tragedy of the Black Hole, and as the average Englishman, at home, if not in India itself, derives his impression of Indian History from Macaulay's Essays, the event of 1756 will never be rivaled in public interest. If, however, it had fallen to Macaulay to describe the massacres at Patna in 1763, there can be no doubt that he would have told a tale which in terror and attrocity would have exceeded even that of the sufferings of Holwell and his companions. For while it may be contended Suraj-ud-daula was in a secondary sense only responsible for the bungling which led to the Black Hole disaster, no such escape is possible for the perpetrator of the massacre of 1763. In a letter to Warren Hastings, dated August 29, 1776, Mir Kasim Khan, in pleading for pardon and permission "to return to his home and hearth with a view to proceeding finally on a pilgrimage to the holy shrines," gave his own version of the circumstances leading to the massacres of Patna, and attempted to lay the burden on the shoulders of the late Mir Jafar, whom, he contended, had intrigued with Sumroo for the murder of the English in order that he (Mir Kasim) might be so ruined in the consideration of the English, that all future opportunities of a reconciliation between the Company and himself might be cut off.[1] With this plea we need only contrast the words which Mir Kasim wrote to Major Adams, on the 9th of September 1763, (after the murder of Amyatt): "Know of a certain that I will cut off the heads of Mr. Ellis and the rest of your chiefs, and send them to you.[2]" The unfortunate victims were not all slain on the same day, and this circumstance in itself proves the deliberation with which these murders of helpless prisoners were accomplished. That the crime was carried out by a European renegade is a circumstance which adds to the horror of the story.

1. PATNA TO A. D. 1757.

Even in India there are but few places so rich in historical memories as Patna. Beneath the soil, watered by the blood of Mir Kasim's victims, lie the ruins of the ancient Buddhist capital, Pataliputra, the greatness of which had been foretold by the Buddha a few months before his death. From the Greek Megasthenes in the 4th century B. C. and the Chinese pilgrim Fa Hein in the 5th, we hear of the wonders of Patna's palaces. After long years of obscurity, ruin, and desolation, the great Mahommedan Conqueror Sher Shah (1541) took in the possibilities of that site, protected by the waters of the Ganges and the Sone, and built there a fortress. In 1586 Ralph Fitch visited Patna, and he has left us a description of that "very long and great towne." In 1573 Patna, and an adjoining fortress at Hajipur, were defended by Daud Khan, the head of the Afghan revolt against the Moghul army: and in 1574 Akbar himself came to capture the city, the downfall of which completed the conquest of Bengal. Then came the great days in which Patna was the centre of political life in Bengal; Azim-us-Shan, the grandson of Aurangzeb, held his court there, and gave to the city his own name—Azimabad, which it bears in works such as the *Seir-i-Mutaqherin.* "It is said," writes Mr. O'Malley, "that the young prince aspired to make the city a second Delhi,

---

1. *Calendar of the Persian Correspondence*, 1766-77, Vol. I, p. 180. For the last dealings of Warren Hasting with Mir Kasim see Forrest: *Selections from the Unpublished Records*, Vol. II. pp. 418-9.

2. Vansittart: *Original Papers Relative to the Disturbances in Bengal*, 1759-64.

but this ambition was cut short by the patricidal war which broke out on the death of Aurangzeb in the course of which he met his death (1712) by being swallowed up alive in a quicksand.[3]" In 1620 the English at Surat pushed on their enterprise from Agra to Patna, where the Portuguese, however, had been first in the field: but these early adventures lacked permanency, and it is not till about 1657 that we find anything like an established trade between the English at Hughli and the place they called 'Pattana' or 'Pattnaw' or 'Patenna.' Tavernier, who with Bernier, visited the city in 1666, writes: "the Holland Company have a house there, by reason of their trade in saltpetre, which they refine at a great town called Champar (Chapra). Coming to Patna, we meet the Hollanders in the street returning from Champar, who stopped our coach to salute us. We did not part till we had emptied two bottles of Shiras wine in the open street, which is not taken notice of in that country where people meet with an entire freedom without any ceremony." About 1659, Job Charnock, in the near future the founder of Calcutta, came to Patna, and in a residence of about twenty years, built up the saltpetre trade with such success, that the Company were able to discontinue their purchases on the West Coast and at Masulipatam.[4] From the time, however, of Charnock's removal, the trade languished under the constant oppression of the native authorities, and in 1715 the factory was abandoned, until it was re-established in 1718.

In the year 1701, the Emperor appointed as Diwan of Bengal one Mahomed Kadi, who, in origin, the son of a poor brahmin of the Deccan, had risen from the humble station of an assistant in the revenue department of the Diwan of the Berrars to be Diwan of Hyderabad[5]. Mahomed Kadi, now become Murshid Kuli Khan, was not long in incurring the wrath of the Viceroy Azim-us-shan, and in consequence, departed from Dacca for Muksudabad which now in his honour bore his name—Murshidabad. It was to the *musnud* established by Murshed Kuli Khan that Ali Verdi Khan, Suraj-ud-daula, Mir Jafar, and Mir Kasim in turn succeeded. In 1719 the subah of Bihar was transferred to the Nawabs of Bengal, and, as the administrative Court of the Emperors had now become a thing of the past, it was in future with the Rulers of Murshidabad that the English factors had to deal.

The times were wild ones: wars and rumours of wars incessant: alarms of Mahrattas and Afghan inroads seldom absent, the reality seldom falling short of the hideousness of the reports. In 1741 the great Nawab Ali Vardi Khan, who in the previous year had defeated and dethroned the Nawab Surfuraz Khan (Murshed Kuli Khan's grandson), rebuilt the fortifications of Patna, making the city a place of refuge for all who sought shelter from the pitiless Mahrattas. Five years after this, Mustapha Khan, the Afghan general, revolted, and laid seige to Patna. "A vast number, therefore, of pioneers and labourers was sent for from all parts of the province, an entrenchment was soon thrown up that encompassed all the grounds between the tower of Jaffar Khan's garden and the dyke a wall raised for the security of the suburbs against the waters of a neighbouring lake. A deep ditch was added to the entrenchment, and the earth dug from it served to form a very good rampart without needing any mortar or brick work." Mustapha Khan's attempt failed, and the leader falling into the hands of his conquerors, his quartered body was hung in triumph on the four gates of Patna city.

In 1746 Rajhuji Bhansla, the Mahratta Chief, in alliance with the turbulent Afghans, fled before the arms of Ali Vardi Khan, leaving behind him a "country totally ruined." But the great Nawab was to find by bitter experience that a man's worst foes are they of his own household. His son-in-law and naib at Patna in 1748 entered into an alliance with the lawless Afghans

3. *Bengal District Gazetteers Vol. VII, Patna* 1907 p. 24.

4. *Bengal Past and Present* Vol. I, Art. "The Founder of Calcutta." The earliest English factory was not in the city but at Singia.

5. Mozumdar: *The Musnud of Murshidabad* p. 21.

of Darbhanga, but Zain-ud-din was doomed to perish at the hands of his faithless allies. His wife Amina Begum, Ali Vardi Khan's daughter, was "for seventeen days forced to listen to the cries of her father-in-law, tortured by every horrible device known to Oriental cruelty, to reveal the place where his treasure lay hid. Then for well nigh a year she spent anxious days a prisoner in the enemy's camp, waiting for the approach of her father's army that hurried along the way. Rescued at last, she returned with Ali Vardi Khan to Murshidabad, and there for seven years set all her hopes upon her son Suraj-ud-daulah, scheming to secure for him the kingdom on her father's death." The pictures drawn of Patna in that awful year 1748 recall to remembrance that terrible description of our own mother land in the days of King Stephen, when men said openly "that Christ and his saints slept." "The insurgents" sacked the city and its suburbs, looted treasures, dishonored women and children, and desolated a whole world:" so writes the author of the *Riyaza-u-Salatin*. At Kali Sarai, near where stands the present railway station at Fatwa, Ali Vardi Khan crushed the revolt effectually, but only to find that his grandson, whom he had petted and spoiled, had risen in revolt, and made a futile attempt to seize Patna.

Previous to Suraj-ud-dawlah's march on Calcutta, the English had abandoned their factory at Patna, and the French had established themselves there in full strength. For the story of Monsr. Law's retreat from Murshidabad to Patna, the reader must be referred to Mr. S. C. Hill's *Three Frenchmen in Bengal*. In July 1757 Mr. Pearkes re-opened the English Factory at Patna. It may be said that after the event of Plassey, Patna is once again the pivot round which the history of the times revolves.

---

2. MILITARY EVENTS, 1757—1761.

At the time of the defeat and assassination of Suraj-ud-daula the Governor of Patna was a Hindu officer, Ramnarain by name, who owing his power and advancement to Ali Vardi Khan, was by the strongest ties of gratitude committed to the cause of the ill-fated Nawab Suraj-ud-daula. Ramnarain who was, as Mr. Hill says "no lover of Mir Jafar, and was not yet acquainted with Clive," allowed Law, the fugitive French Chief of Cossimbazar, to pass Patna and escape into the province of Oudh. Forcing his way with the greatest difficulty, Coote, who had taken charge of the expedition, which Clive himself had at first intended to command, followed without success on the track of the fugitive French. The story of Coote's transactions is an exceedingly interesting one: but we cannot pause to trace it even in the barest outline in this place. Law made good his escape: and Coote, who at one time had thought of capturing the citadel of Patna by force of arms from Ramnarain, in the end came to an understanding—the latter swearing fealty to Mir Jafar, on the express promise of an English guarantee for his honour, safety, and position. It was no doubt the consideration of this solemn recognition which made Coote so resolute, and Carnac also, in opposing Vansittart's policy in regard to Ramnarian. In February 1758, Clive and his army marched through Patna, and encamped at "the Company's gardens" at Bankipur. It would require more space than can be here afforded to detail the intrigues and counter-intrigues. In the end, the Nawab appointed his son Mir Miran to the Government of Patna —"a mere honorary appointment which gave him a claim to certain presents or fees," and Ramnarian (who however paid a *doceur* of 7 lakhs) was installed as Naib, *i. e.* the actual Governor of the Province. Clive next devoted his attention to secure for the Company the farm of the revenues on the all important saltpetre commerce. He then set to work to raise a third battalion of sepoys—a corps, afterwards commanded by Captain Turner, the destruction of which in 1763 is a part of the present story. On May the 27th Clive left Patna, and (at Bar) secured from the Nawab further undertakings on behalf of the safety of Ramnarian.

In 1760 fresh troubles came in view. At the invitation of some rebellious zemindars and military officers, the Mogul Prince, Ali Gohar, made his appearance on the scene. On his way southward, news reached him of the death of his father, and he at once assumed the title of Emperor and the name of Shah Alam. Clive, who left Bengal for England on the 25th February 1760, in the previous December had despatched Major Caillaud with a small army to meet the invader. But Shah Alam reached Patna before Caillaud and, on February 9th, Ramnarain marched out of Patna to meet the enemy. The story of the battle in "the plains of Mussempore" has been well told by Broome : but it is the story of the retreat that concerns us because it introduces to us in the most favourable light the man who was to be one of the very few survivors from Mir Kasim's clutches in 1763—Surgeon William Fullarton. The English forces, whose orders confined them to the protection of Ramnarain, were but some 700 or 800 men. Ramnarain, who had haughtily declined to remain with the English, finding the battle against him, appealed to Captain Cochrane, the English Commander, to send him support, and Cochrane at once marched with four companies of sepoys to the Raja's support. Let Broome continue the story :—

"This unwise division of the English force caused its destruction ; the party under Captain Cochrane forced their way to the Rajah and covered his retreat ; but being attacked on all sides they were overwhelmed by numbers, and the only three officers present, Captain Cochrane, Ensign Winclebeck, and Mr. Barwell, who served as a volunteer, were slain : the sipahis, now left without a leader, were discouraged, and Kamghur Khan's Cavalry, making a desperate rush, charged in upon them, and the whole party were cut to pieces—1 sergeant and 25 sipahis alone succeeding in fighting their way back to the European detachment. These last, supported by the other Companies of sipahis had also been severely assailed, but continued to hold their ground : the officer left in charge of the infantry, as also the subaltern in command of the Artillery, who appears to have been Lieutenant Buck were both killed ; the only European officer now surviving was Dr. W. Fullarton, the Surgeon of the Agency, who assumed the command. Finding that the day was completely lost, this little party commenced their retreat to the city, surrounded by the enemy, but by the coolness and steadiness of their conduct keeping the latter at a respectful distance. One of the gun carriages having broken down, they were compelled to spike it and leave it on the field, but the tumbrel of the other having upset, Dr. Fullarton halted the party, deliberately righted it, and then resumed his march : by their cool and daring behaviour this remnant of the party succeeded in making good their retreat to Patna." (Page 282.)

After the battle of Seerphore, which but for Mir Miran's procrastinations and jealousy of Col. Caillaud, might have proved decisive against Shah Alam, the latter retreated in the direction of Midnapore, and Mir Miran and Caillaud followed in pursuit, forming a junction with the Nawab at Mongolkote on April 4th, 1760. It would be tedious to follow the incidents of this difficult campaign. On April the 10th the Emperor set back to Patna, and falling in with Law in Behar, he shortly after proceeded to invest the city. In the course of the siege, Fullarton once again distinguished himself by his bravery. After a desperate defence, the little garrison was on the point of despair, when at noon-day of the 28th of April, to their surprise and unspeakable delight, the guard on the walls beheld an English reinforcement approaching. "The welcome aid consisted of Captain Knox's little party, who, in the incredibly short space of 13 days, had arrived from Burdwan, a distance of 300 miles, under a burning sun, having crossed the Ganges twice, and experienced great difficulties and privation."

The story of Knox's exploits is wildly adventurous even when compared with those of Clive. A successful night attack of Kamghur Khan's camp led to the latter removing his army to a considerable distance, and after a few days the Imperial Army raised the siege. Patna being thus relieved, Knox turned his attention to Kuddum Hussain, the rebellious chief of Purnea, who was marching with a powerful army, to join the Emperor. Assisted by the gallant Shitab Roy, Knox with a mere handful of men achieved wonders. Near to Bheerpore he fell in with the enemy, who after a hard fight, despite their overwhelming numbers, were put to flight, leaving 400 dead on the field, and 13 elephants and 8 pieces of canon in Knox's hand; 16 Europeans only were killed, and a proportionate number of sepoys. On 22nd June, Caillaud and Mir Miran arrived, and Knox and his men, who had followed in pursuit of the foe, returned to garrison Patna.

The pursuit of Kuddum Hussain was prosecuted by Caillaud, and might have met with success but for the tragedy which occurred on the night of July 2nd, when, in a violent storm, the "young Nawab," Mir Miran, was killed by lightning After seizing the town of Bettiah, Caillaud and his forces returned to Patna. Of this officer little more is to be said. Had he remained in Bengal history might perhaps have taken a somewhat different course, for he was no friend to Mir Jafar, and he was one of those who received a considerable bounty from Mir Kasim in connection with the revolution of 1760. He handed over the command at Patna to Captain Knox on August 31st, and reached Calcutta on September 10th 1760. On October 20th Caillaud was at Murshedabad superintending the *coup d'etat*, and, after all had been accomplished, he returned to Patna, accompanied by one who has a large part to play in these pages—Major John Carnac.[6]

We shall not attempt to follow Carnac in his victorious struggle with the Emperor Shah Alam and his French and other allies; for we must now proceed with the more purely political events which led up to the tragedy which the *Diaries of the Three Surgeons* describe. Thoroughly defeated by Carnac, the Emperor on February 6th, 1761 came into the English camp, to seek the best terms that could be obtained. In the old letters given here it is Shah Alam who must be understood by such expressions as "His Majesty," "the King," etc.

---

3. THE PARTY FORMED AGAINST GOVERNOR VANSITTART.

In February 1760, after Forde's decisive victory over the Dutch at Biddera, Clive felt himself free to leave Bengal for England, and for the time the chair of Government was occupied by Holwell, the hero of the Black Hole, but apparently only as a temporary arrangement. After Holwell's departure, Peter Amyatt, the then chief at Patna, who in seniority would have succeeded to the chair, was passed over in favour of Henry Vansittart, who arrived in Calcutta from Madras in July. On October 27th took place, quietly and without any loss of life, the revolution which placed Mir Kasim Khan on the *musnud*, to which Clive had raised Mir Jafar after the battle of Plassey.

The supersession of Bengal servants by a stranger from Madras had been bitterly resented. The natural leader of the disaffected party was, of course, Amyatt, but he seems to have been a person of an amiable disposition, and, according to Vansittart it was one Fullarton, who prompted a peaceful man to the conflict. On the 8th January 1761, Amyatt caused a minute to be entered on the proceedings of the Select Committee, in which in the strongest terms—"breach of faith," "odium," "assisted to dethrone a man we were bound to support by the most solemn ties divine and human" etc.—he expressed, on behalf of himself and Messrs. Ellis and Smyth, an entire

---

6 "Major Carnac," writes Broome, "had embarked for England with Lord Clive, but on arrival at St. Helena he received intelligence of his appointment to the command of the Bengal Troops, with the rank of Major, in the room of Major Cailland, who was at the same time promoted to the rank of Lieutenant-Colonel, and decided to return to the coast, and assume command of the Madras Army in succession to Colonel Lawrence. Major Carnac immedately returned to Bengal, where he arrived in the middle of October Vansittart, however, directed that Colonel Cailland should for a time retain the general command, as the senior officer, and because his services and experience were required in the settlement of important measure then in contemplation." Cailland left Patna finally on December 31st 1760.

disapprobation of the late revolution.[7] In replying to this minute, the Governor dealt out hard measures to Ellis.

> "That Mr. Smyth should subscribe to this opinion is not to be wondered at because he subscribed to one of the like nature of Mr. Verelst's, in consultation of the 8th November, without having read any of the preceedings; but that Mr. Ellis should subscribe to it, after signifying his approbation of the measures[8] in many letters which have been written on the subject; and particularly in one from the Select Committee to the Governor and Colonel Caillaud, dated the 24th of November, is somewhat surprising, and gives fresh reason to apprehend, what has long been suspected, that other persons, not in the Company's service, nor having any regard for the Company, are consulted upon affairs which do not belong to them; by which unfortunately they gain an ascendency over the minds of better men than themselves; and this authority they exert to the utmost, to the purpose of making divisions in the settlement, and more particularly in the Council. It is only such persons as those, that can reflect upon the late measures, as a breach of all ties, human and divine; a reproach which nothing can merit, but a premeditated intention to do some great ill."

To this Ellis replied, on January 11th, 1711. His previous utterances were but "a complimentary congratulation", but "his sentiments with regard to the revolution have never altered, nor have they been kept a secret." "The reflection of his being influenced in his opinion by others, though not of so good a turn of mind as himself, is a compliment to his morals, at the expense of his capacity, which being merely personal, and quite foreign to the subject in hand, might well have been spared: and in answer thereto, he only wishes, for the good of this settlement, others in power were as little influenced in the management of public affairs, by the opinion of those about them."

Vansittart in his *Narrative* suggests that the original cause of Ellis' disaffection was due to the fact that, on his return from England, Ellis had claimed the chiefship at Patna, to which Mr. McGuire had been appointed two months before—a claim Vansittart considered to be unreasonable. Major Carnac had also been "violently offended at my expressing a desire that Colonel Caillaud, who had been present at all the debates of the Secret Committee, and had been particularly charged with the execution of their resolutions, should remain in command at Patna till their views were fulfilled." (Vol. 1. p. 160).

---

4. THE OPPOSITION OF COL. EYRE COOTE AND MAJOR CARNAC TO THE POLICY OF THE GOVERNOR.

The rule of Mir Kasim Khan, at its start, was full of bright promises, and in fact he was able to produce so large a sum for the support of the forces, that the Government at Calcutta were able to remit two and half lakhs to Madras, which sum arrived at that place "very opportunely for service of the army before Pondichery:" In the meanwhile Carnac's successes against the

---

7. Vansittart: A *Narrative of the Transactions in Bengal* (1766) Vol. 1, p. 106 *et seq.* or *Original Papers* Vol. 1, pp. 67, *et seq.* The minute goes so far to assert that the cession of the provinces of Midnapore, Burdwan, and Chittagong will be an entirely imaginary advantage. The real grounds for condemning the Revolution are given by Elphinstone in his *Rise of the British Power in the East* and it is interesting to contrast them with those given in Amyatt's minute.

8. Ellis had written on October 25th 1760 to the Governor: "It is with much pleasure I hear of tranquility in the city: such a revolution with so little disturbance scarce ever happened, and I dare say, Sir, there will be nothing wanting, on your part, to place this tranquility on a lasting and solid foundation." Verelst's resolution referred to will be found in the *Original Paper*. Vol. 1, pp. 60-61: it is based on the fact that the whole Council had not been consulted. To this Vansittart replied that the affair "absolutely required secrecy, and that it is expressly for the conduct of such affairs that the Court of Directors has thought proper to appoint a Select Committee." Verelst was shortly after sent to arrange for the settlement of Chittagong.

Shahzada, and Captain White's against the rebellious Raja of Beerbhum had in some measure brought peace to the troubled country. But a new cause of distraction was almost at once found in the person of Ramnarain, who, as we have seen, had been intrusted with the Governorship of Patna by the deposed Nawab, and who, being on unfriendly terms with the new Nawab, looked to the English for protection. Caillaud, having been ordered to Pondichery, the Military Command at Patna fell on Carnac, and however much he may have been influenced by the pique Vansittart ascribes to him, it is clear that the Major was prepared to resent any deviation from what he took regarded as policy of his great military chief, Lord Clive. Caillaud had been instructed by the Select Committee to extend his protection to Ramnarain in case of the Nabab's making any attempt against the person or honour of the latter. On February 9th, 1761 the Select Committee informed Carnac:

> "We believe such an injunction at this time unnecessary, as the present Nabob seems to be well inclined towards Ramnarain," but they at the same time confirmed their resolution "to have the same regard to the former engagements in his favour". "As to Rajebullub," they continued, "we can have no reasonable objection to a fair examination of his accounts by the Nabob, or such person as he shall appoint; that a just statement being made of all the monies he has received, for defraying the charges of the troops under his command, together with a due enquiry of what number of troops have really been kept up, and how much every one has been paid: the balance that has been found due may then be discharged, and Rajebullub be employed again, as the Nabob thinks proper. This the Nabob declares is all that he asks, and in this (as it is just and reasonable) you will yield to him all the necessary assistance."

To these instructions the Major replied, on February 24th, in a letter which Vansittart in his *Narrative* characterises in severe terms—"unbecoming and arrogant," "vanity and intemperance," "prejudices which he had entertained against the Nabob." The letter is as follows:

> "You may depend upon my giving the Nabob all the assistance in my power, to settle everything in the province in the best manner; I will also very readily lend my assistance in adjusting the payment of that part of the troops under Rajebullub, as far as he means to act fairly by them; but should he expect any support from me in acts of injustice, he will be much mistaken. The English forces, which I have the honour of commanding, shall never be employed as instruments of violence and oppression.
>
> "Your directions, in regard to Ramnarain, shall be religiously observed: I could not have received any order from you with more pleasure than this, of protecting a person, for whom I know Colonel Clive had a peculiar regard, and who himself deserves much at the hands of the English, on account of the attachment he has all along shown them, however ill he might be disposed to the Nabob."

Early in March, the Nabob and the Major met at Bykuntpore. It is impossible to read Mir Kasim's correspondence without being struck by his very considerable skill as a letter-writer, and his ability in putting forth an *ex parte* statement of his own case in which nearly everything, but the essential points, receive more than adequate justice. If Mir Kasim were to be judged on the merits of his letters only, we should at least have a sneaking regard for him. It will be well to place the Nabob's and the Major's account of what took place at Bykuntpore in parallel columns: it will be seen that the former suppresses the fact that he himself had caused the withdrawal of Ramnarain and Rajebullub from the country of the rebellious Kamghur Khan.

Carnac's Letter.—March 6, 1761.

The Nabab continues encamped at Bykuntpore, about six or seven coss off, where I have waited upon him; whatever good qualities he may have, courage is not one of them: he betrays a most shameful fear of the Shahzada, though the unhappy Prince is reduced so low, as to be much more an object of pity than of fear. Not thinking himself sufficiently secure with the large force he brought up with him, he sent for, without acquainting me, both Ramnarain and Rajebullub with their forces, whom I had directed to remain in Camgar Cawn's country, with a detachment from our army, under the command of Captain Champion. I no sooner heard of this but recalled Captain Champion likewise, which has given the Nabab great offence, so great, that he asked me in the publick Durbar, whether I would comply with the contents of the letter he brought me from the President. I answered that I would, as far as I was well persuaded that Mr. Vansittart expected from me, who did not mean that I was to pay an implicit obedience. I further told him that the direction of the English forces was left with me; and that it was not reasonable any part of them should remain in a country with which they were wholly unacquainted, after he had withdrawn his own people. I have, however, at his own request, ordered Captain Champion's detatchment to halt awhile at Behar, but shall call them in entirely, unless he sends out a body of his own troops to act in conjunction with them; the neglect whereof will infallibly bring Camgar Cawn out of his hills again.

The Nawab's Letter, received March 13, 1761.

On the 26th of Rejub, I arrived at Bykuntpore, where I had the pleasure of meeting Major Carnac, Maharajah Ramnarin, and Maharajah Rajebullub. Among other things the Major told me that he had sent for the troops which were at Gamty, in the zemindarree of Camgar Cawn. I replied that to chastize Camgar Cawn was no difficult matter; but that it was not proper to recall the troops, belonging to the Company and myself, in so much haste, from the place where they were stationed. This he did not consent to do; but replied that he would certainly send for his English troops. I delivered your letter to him. When he perused it, he said that Mr. Vansittart is two hundred coss from hence; and that he would do whatever he thought advisiable. I was persuaded that he would have acted according to your directions, and did not imagine that he would have given me such an answer. The Nabab next asked me, whether I looked upon him as Subahdar of the provinces, and was willing to assist him as such. In answer to which I plainly told him, I would give him all the assistance I could, confident with honour and justice; that further I would not do for him or any man. The very question gives me room to suspect he has same unreasonable demands to make of me; should this be the case, he will undergo the mortification of a denial. I parted from the Nabab yesterday evening. We were both, you will judge, pretty much dissatisfied with each other; he with me, for speaking my mind so freely to him, a thing very unprecedented in this country; and I with him, for the delays and obstruction he is likely to cause to our military operations.

Vansittart, in his *Narrative* (1766), talks of "the slights which the Major put upon the Nabab at this interview," but a letter of the Select Committee (Vansittart, Amyatt, Ellis and Sumner) while deploring any lack of harmony between the Major and the Nawab, censures the latter's conduct in sending for Ramnarain and Rajebullub as "a very imprudent step and much to be blamed." While asserting that "the disposition of the army, and the determination on all military matters should rest with our commanding officer," the Committee laid it down that "in everything respecting the regulation of the country and the collection of the revenues," the Major subject to more urgent considerations (*e. g.*, the safety of the troops), should be guided by the Nawab. "We think," they added, "this distinction is sufficiently clear, and flatter ourselves that no disputes can hereafter arise."[9] In this expectation they were destined to be sadly and completely disappointed.

A few weeks after at this interview at Bykuntpore, Colonel Coote arrived at Calcutta, and on April 22nd he set out to assume the command of the army at Patna. His instructions from the Select Committee, dated the day previous, read as follows :

> "We are advised by Major Carnac, that there is a difference between the Nabab and Ramnarain, relative to the accounts of the Patna province. We hope this may be amicably and reasonably adjusted, and request that you will give your assistance towards it as much as possible. As Ramnarain has been remarkably steady in his allegiance with the Company, and received from Colonel Clive particular assurances of his protection with respect to his person, fortune, and government, we recommend you to secure him against all attempts of oppression or injustice, and further that the Government of Patna be preserved for him, if it is his inclination to continue in it. It is needless for us to add, that it will be far more agreeable to all parties, if that can be done by representing to the Nabab the obligations we are under to Ramnarain, and preventing by that means the necessity of any forcible means."

On May the 8th, Carnac, in consequence of Coote's arrival, wrote to the Select Committee expressing a desire to be allowed to return to Calcutta with a view to proceeding to England, but on Coote's arrival at Calcutta, the Major finding the views of his superior officer were coincident with his own, postponed his intended departure. I must pass as rapidly as possible over the events which occurred between Coote's arrived at Patna, and the recall of Coote and Carnac. It is somewhat important, however, to notice that McGuire, the Company's Chief at Patna, plays a very minor part on every occasion of importance, but that his sympathies were on the whole cast on the side of the Nawab. Passing over many materials of lesser importance, we come to a letter from the Nawab to the Governor, dated June 16th 1761.

> Since the arrival of Colonel Coote, agreeably to your directions, esteeming his will worthy of my principal attention, and regarding our mutual friendship, I have never been deficient in acting agreeably thereto. After his arrival here, he spoke to me in the following manner concerning the King's affairs, "that as long as he should remain here, I should consent to allow him a lack of rupees monthly for his expenses, and that when he should go to Delly, I should consent to dismiss him with twelve lacks of rupees and a few troops." These articles, for the Colonel's satisfaction, I was under a necessity of consenting to ; and I went to his Majesty, and told him I would be answerable for these conditions ; but he would not consent to it. Afterwards the Colonel directed me to pay, besides what I before gave him, fifty thousand rupees. Agreeable, therefore, to the Colonel's desire, I gave him the said sum by the means of Maharajah Ramnarain, besides what I paid before. His Majesty made no stay here, but determined to proceed to Delly, and is now on his march that way. When his Majesty was departing, I spoke to the Colonel concerning the obtaining of the Sunnuds ; but he was not satisfied and forbade me. I was under the necessity of acquiescing in his pleasure, and deferred it, nor mentioned it again. Roy Shitabroy, who is appointed for the negociation of affairs at his Majesty's

9. *Original Papers*, Vol. 1, p. 81.

court, always endeavours to throw things into confusion. I frequently desired the Colonel to dismiss him as an incendiary, and appoint another in his place, but he would not listen to it. Ever since the Colonel came here, to this time, I have regarded what he said and directed as of the greatest consequence, making it a principal point to establish a friendship between us, and to gain his affection. According to the rules of friendship, I have observed all the customs and forms in entertainments of eating and reciprocal visits more attentively and more heartily with him than I ever did with any other person. In every respect, I have done everything to please and satisfy him, and entered into mutual engagements with him; notwithstanding which behaviour, he has not consented to a single thing I have requested of him. Agreeable to what you wrote to me concerning Maharajah Ramnarain's affairs, I spoke to the Colonel, and, at his recommendation, appointed Maharajah Rajebullub to examine the accounts. Golam Aly Cawn and the said Maharajah, went backwards and forwards to the Kella for fifteen or sixteen days together; but Ramnarain neither gave them a single paper nor a writer to attend them. Afterwards the Colonel came and said to me: "We Europeans do not understand the country accounts; I will send the Maharajah "Ramnarain to you, he shall not be dismissed, but you may examine the accounts yourself." This I would not consent to: nevertheless, the next day, he sent him to me, contrary to my will, with Mr. Watts. Since that day to the present moment, he (Ramnarain) protracts the time in going backwards and forwards, and fixing the time for preparing his papers, but he has not produced a single cowry, nor delivered over a rupee's worth of the country; though I have complained, no one would listen to me, nor give me redress. Ever since my arrival here, the English seapoys have been stationed at the gates of the city, and would not permit my people to pass and repass. Mr. McGuire being somewhat indisposed, I went to see him at the factory; and from thence I went to the Colonel, and sat down and conversed with him. He declared that on Tuesday, the 12th of Zeccada, I would go to the Kella, and on Friday the 15th, cause the Cootba to be read, and siccas to be struck in the name of his Majesty. This I agreed to do and returned home. When the officers of my troops heard that I was going into the Kella, they represented that they should have frequent occasion to come to me, in order to lay their requests and petitions before me; and that till the seapoys, etc., were taken off, they could not pass and repass without interruption; that when Meer Mahomed Jaffar Alli Cawn, and Nafir-ool-Moolk, deceased, resided in the Killa, the seapoy guards were not upon the gates; and that until they were taken off, they should not be able to pass; considering, therefore, that the seapoys were men of low disposition, frequently opposing men of credit in passing, and presenting their pieces to them, and that many of my people were proud and haughty, so that disputes may arise and disturbances be created, I therefore wrote a letter to the Colonel, requesting he would take off the seapoys from the gates, and then I would go into the Kella. Upon the receipt of this letter, which contained no more than what I have here mentioned, the Colonel was very angry and flew into such a passion, that he said he would send for the King again, and told Golam Aly Cawn, who was then present, that he would not take the guards off the gates, and that I might send troops to drive them off. Since the day the Colonel arrived here, he has declared to me, that I must comply with everything that he shall recommend; and accordingly, he has since told be in person, and by messages brought by Mr. Watts[10]

10. Hugh Watts—a son of Watts, who had carried on the secret negotiations with Mir Jafar before Plassey. His mother was the famous Calcutta lady afterwards known as the "Begum Johnson."

and Sheik Cumaul, that: "I must appoint Nundcoomar to the Foujedaree[11] of Hooghly, give the government of Poornea to the son of Aly Cooley Cawn, restore Mazuffer Aly (who plundered Masir-ol-Moolk's jewels to the amount of eight lakhs of rupees) to the Zemindaree of Carrackpoor, restore Camgur Cawn to the Zemindarree of Mey, and regulate the Zemindarrees of Radshay and Dinagepore, according to his pleasure.[12]

Though I desired the Colonel to appoint a muttasedee[13] to examine the accounts of my eight months' government, and let me free: he would not listen to it. All my hopes of reliance are on your friendship and attachments to your engagements. This is the only consolation I have under my present afflictions; it is the dependence that I have upon your word that keeps me alive, without this, it would be impossible to survive them. My hopes were, from the revenues of this province to pay my debt to the Company and reduce the number of my forces; but nothing is yet done; I apprehend the seapoys will assemble, as in Meer Jafar Aly Cawn's time, and put my life in danger, and bring shame and dishonour upon my family. In the eight months of my government, I have scarce had leisure to drink a little water. I have not had a minute's time to eat or enjoy sleep. The four months that I have been here, involved in troubles, I have not enjoyed the least happiness, except in the confidence I have in your friendship. My shame and hishonour are completed, and I have no one to complain to but you; I hope you will speedily write me in what manner I can extricate myself from these difficulties, and establish my credit and reputation. Every particular of what I have now wrote has befallen me, God is my witness, and Mr. McGuire is acquainted with every circumstance. I am sorry that you, who are my patron and the partaker of my afflictions, should at this time be at such a distance, and that so much time should be taken up in writing and receiving letters. The rains are come on, and the sepoys' wages daily increase. The affairs of the country fall every day into greater confusion, and everything contributes to make my life a burthen to me; my hopes are in your favour; for God's sake make no delay; if you do, my affairs

---

11. Foujedari [Phausdari] The office of the native chief Magistrate of a large district called a Chuckla.

12. To these charges, Coote replied (July 17th 1761): "The Nawab further accuses me of having endeavoured to oblige him to make up matters with Comgar Cawn and the Carrackpoor Rajah. I declare, I never mentioned them to him in any other light than that, if he could not by any means take them, to make up matters with them; and that I particularly refused to see their Vackeels, and never had any correspondence with them, but by two letters, which I wrote them by the Nawab's desire, copies of which have been transmitted to the President. With regard to the Dinagepore people, I was petitioned by the sons of the late Rajah (whose country had been taken from them by the Nawab after taking a nuzzur of ten lacks of rupees) requesting that I would speak with the Nawab on their behalf, and deliver their petition to him, which was all the part I acted in that affair. With respect to the Rajah of Radshay, Mr. Batson desired I would endeavor to serve him with the Nawab, as he had been fleeced by the Royroyan, and his country taken from him. I accordingly represented it to him; since which representation, that poor unhappy man (though seventy years of age) has been tied up by the heels, and flogged with rattans almost to death. This shocking piece of cruelty, not being thought sufficient, he was put in irons and remained in that situation, till Mr. Batson, through his humanity, with difficulty, by his interest, got him freed from his shackles; but the poor old man still continues a prisoner. As to Mirza Kelly Aly, I never mentioned him to the Nawab, nor has any body done it by authority from me The only person whose interest I urged was the unhappy brother of Meer Jaffier, with whom I was formerly acquainted, and whom I found, on my journey to Patna, at Ragemaul, starving with a large family. I begged the Nawab to do something for him; and he ordered him 1,000 rupees *per* month, chiefly through the intercession of Rajebullub, who, by my request, used his interest on that occasion, but that poor man has not profited by this in the least, having hitherto not received a single rupee. As there was a report spread that the Foujedar of Hooghly was to be turned out, Mr. Watts mentioned, in a private discourse with Rajebullub, that if the Nawab would give that post to Nundcomar, it might be the means of obliging some gentleman, whose friendship might be acceptable to him; and this was really hinted from a friendly view towards the Nabob." *A Narrative*, etc. Vol. 1 pp. 246—9. In a footnote, Vansittart says that the old man, whose sufferings from the rattans Coote describes, was not the Rajah of Radshay but the dewan to the Rani. "This country, he adds" (the richest in Bengal) had been put under the inspection of the officers of the Durbar by Jaffer Aly Cawn, who managed the collections jointly with the Dewan. In this same state it now remained." For the benefit of the general reader it may be explained that the "Royroyan" was the principal officer under the Nawab as Dewan or chief revenue officer of the province.

13. Muttaseddee. Vansittart defines as "Properly an officer of state. A term applied in common to any man, who has charge of accounts, either of the Government, or of any person of consequence."

are utterly ruined. Now this remains, that you, who are concerned in my welfare, come here yourself, or send for me to relate my sorrows to you.

[*In the Nawab's own hand.*]

All affairs here are at an end, and the ruinous situation of my affairs at this place has rendered my case desperate. I have wrote to you every particular, I hope from your benevolence, that you will consider every syllable, and speedily redress my complaints.[14]

This letter, exaggerated as are its terms, and inaccurate as to its statements of fact, at least serves to show that the Nawab was under the gloomiest apprehension as to his situation.

Although the Mogul Empire had long since ceased to be a power, yet its continued existence was now and for many years to come the rung painted on a wall from which the whole chain of jurisdiction in India depended. Mir Jafar had received the Mogul's sunnud, but Mir Kasim was still without that credential then deemed so essential to the constitutional exercise of rule. Bitterly the Nawab complained that the Colonel stood in his way and prevented his obtaining the desired "sunnud for the subahdaree."

Things were ripe for a crisis. It has been seen that the Colonel had requested the Nawab to come into the Fort, and cause the Cootba to be read, and the siccas struck in the name of His Majesty. In a letter dated June 15th, the Nawab informed Coote that he had fully resolved to comply with the requisition, but that, as his "Rissaldars and Jemmatdars" resented the continuance of low caste seapoys (Telingas) at the gates, they refused to accompany him, and that he himself therefore was unable to enter the Fort. The letter in itself and the manner in which it was sent caused some surprise to the Colonel, and the more so when it was discovered that the Nawab had been in consultation with his officers, and that the guard on the Nawab's camp had been doubled. On the night of the 16th when "Colonel Coote made an entertainment for the Dutch and was making merry," and his "guards were stationed all around the Killa, came an alarm—originating, so Mir Kasim asserted, and McGuire believed, from Ramnarain—that the Nawab intended to attack the city. It will be well to place Coote's and Mir Kasim's account of what took place in parallel columns.

COOTE.

On the 10th of June, in the evening, having had different reports brought me concerning the Nabob's proceedings, I told Captain Eiser, I intended paying him a visit next morning to endeavour to settle matters with him; and at supper time, desired that gentleman to order the troopers, and my usual attendants to be ready a little after daylight. About six o'clock next morning, I set out from my quarters to the Nabob's (which is about two coss) with about twenty-four European Cavalry, and one Company of seapoys, which happened, at that time, to be a fewer number than usually attended me when I went upon public visits; and I sent Mr. Watts on before, to let the Nabob know I was coming on to wait on him. By the time I arrived at his tents it

MIR KASIM.

About 12 at night, Maharajah Ramnarain collected his people together, and sent word to the Colonel that I had got my troops in readiness to attack the kella in the morning, and that I would spare neither of them. The Colonel, being deceived by the snare, got his people ready. My Hircarras brought me intelligence of it, but I gave no credit to it. This morning Mr. Watts entered my private apartment, which is near the Zenana, calling out: 'Where is the Nawab?' and then stopt. After him Colonel Coote, in a great passion with his horsemen, peons, seepoys and others, with a cocked pistol in each hand, came swearing into my tent. It so happened that I was asleep in the Zenana, and none of my guards were present. How shall I express the unbecom-

14. *Narrative* Vol. 1. p. 207, *et seq.*

was near seven o'clock. The Nabob, I find, accuses me of going in a violent manner, through his tents; on the contrary, the place where I alighted from my horse was near the Durbar tent, and the place where I had always alighted; and upon seeing Mr. Watts, I asked him where the Nawab was? who replied he was asleep in his zanana; and, as I had reason to suspect from my intelligence, the last 24 hours, that his intentions were not the best, I therefore alighted, took my pistols out of my holsters, for my own security (as I seldom ride with a sword), but declare they were not cocked; and I affirm that I went no further than the Durbar tent, where I sat down for a little time; still finding the Nabob did not come, I desired Captain Eiser to order two troopers to see that no body of troops came in at the back part of the tent; and I now declare that no one was placed on his Zenana. As the Nawab did not come, I went away.

ing manner in which the Colonel went about from tent to tent, with 35 horsemen and 200 seepoys, calling out: "Where is the Nawab." He left some of his people at the Zenana and Dewans conna, and went towards the fourth tent. The eunuch of the serai and Mr. Watts prevented his entering, saying the Nabob is asleep, and this is the private tent of the Zenana. The Colonel returned, and proceeded through my whole army, and seeing every one without arms or any preparations, went back to the kella. This base man [*i. e.* Ramnarain] is ungrateful, treacherous, and only intent on mischief; and to suppose such a wicked man, has not any fear of God, and has even forgotten himself, is to give cause for mutual animosities. ....

....

Commenting on the Nawab's letter, and, not having as yet heard the Colonel's version of the facts, McGuire wrote to Vansittart: "I foresaw in same degree the bad consequences of giving such ample powers to your Commander-in-Chief. Few men can brook the losing any part of the authority wherewith they are vested; and fewer still, who can support that authority with moderation. If you cannot come yourself, as I find the gentleman at Madras will not send the regiment, have you not the power to re-call him, and confine the Major to military operations only?" The Council at Calcutta, however, on reading the Nawab's and McGuire's letter, determined that Colonel Coote and Major Carnac[15] should be ordered down to Calcutta, leaving at Patna four Companies of infantry and two battalions of seepoys, under the command of Captain Carstairs, and that this officer should act entirely under the orders of the Chief of the Factory.[16]

5. ELLIS BECOMES CHIEF AT PATNA.

Section VII of Vansittart's *Narrative of Transactions in Bengal* is taken up by an attempt to display, from Carnac's own letters, the latters "arrogance and self-opinion, and tendency to subvert all the order of Government, and to keep up the spirit of party." The Major, we are told, was too much encouraged in these insults on the authority of the Board by some of the members themselves,

15. Major Carnac, at the time of these later troubles, was attending Shah Alam on his journey towards Delhi. The "King," as the Mogul was called by the English, on this occasion made an offer of the Diwani of the three provinces. Vansittart was much piqued by the King's habit of addressing most of his correspondence, not to the Governor and Council, but to the Council only—a breach of etiquette which Vansittart attributed to the Major's desire to derrogate from his authority.

16. The authorities in Calcutta acted on the receipt of the Nawab's letters dated June 16th and 17th. Colonel Coote's letter to the Governor and Council was dated July 17th, and he was therefore in a position to protest "I have not been the first person whose actions have been condemned unheard. I, therefore, cannot look upon it as a particular misfortune attending me alone." *Narrative* Vol. 1 p. 243. As to the Nawab's objection to the guards at the gates, the sepoys were a part of the Nawab's army, and they were under orders to stop nobody belonging to his camp from entering and leaving the city. Mir Kasim had avowed his inability to discipline his forces, and Carnac had had a painful experience of the ill-ordered soldiery of Murshidabad. The Colonel had expressed his willingness to put some of the Nawab's own people, together with his own, at the gates.

who not only vindicated all his opinions, but afforded him an argument to disrespect their orders, by signing their dissent to the orders themselves, instead of minuting them on the consultations. It is clear, however, that Carnac was much, if not mainly, influenced by the suspicion that the Governor was about, in disregard of repeated pledges, to withdraw English protection from Ramnarain.

In September 1761, letters arrived from the Court, requiring Messrs. Sumner, McGuire, and Playdell to be dismissed, and soon after this Smith tendered his resignation and sailed for Europe. Their places were taken by John Cartier Warren Hastings, Johnstone and Hay, and Ellis became Chief at Patna, where he arrived about the middle of November. The instructions given to the new Chief at Patna were sharply debated by the Board. Although Ramnarain is not mentioned in them, it was pointed out that "the impropriety of protecting a servant against his masters" was calculated to cause "nothing but jealousy and ill-will between the Nabob and the Company," and it would be "expressly contrary to our engagements with the Nabob." The Agent was not to interfere, directly or indirectly, in any of the affairs of the country government or with the people belonging to it, but to place his armed forces at the Nawab's service whensoever requested. Some of the Board very rightly censured this arrangement by which the Chief was deprived of any right of discretion in regard to the nature of the services on which English troops might be employed. Hastings, while on the whole supporting the Governor, was of opinion that although the Chief should have no power of discretion, yet he should be able to make a representation to the Council, should be think the service required of our troops to be "hurtful to the English character." Carnac thought that Ellis should be allowed power to decide. Amyatt thought the proposed arrangement dishonourable to our masters, an indignity to the Board, and an unprecedented case till the chiefship of Mr. McGuire, and in this view Coote concurred.

With Ellis' arrival at Patna, disputes with the country authorities become so many that it would be hopeless to attempt to recount them here. Among the most earliest and conspicuous instances of these disputes are: the arrest of an officer of the Government named Munseram on a complaint from a Gomastah of the English factory; the seizure of an Armenian, Coja Aratoom, for interference in the Company's saltpetre monopoly, the search of Monghyr Fort for the persons of two deserters. It will, however, be more useful to leave these details of the quarrel on one side, and proceed at once to discuss the question out of which an infinite number of troubles were bound to arise.

6. THE PRIVATE TRADE OF THE COMPANY'S SERVANTS.

In a letter dated January 24th, 1767, Clive and his Council made a remark which, ably and amply, sums up the whole moral of the history of the period we are discussing. "We" they wrote, "now come to your instructions relative to the inland trade, which you very justly consider as the foun- "dation of all the bloodshed, massacres and confusion, which have happened of late years in Bengal."[17] The inland trade referred to here is defined by Vansittart "as trade carried on by private persons, on their own credit and bottom, in commodities produced in the country, and again sold in the same country..........The private trade consists of goods not fit for exportation, but which are again sold in the country; or it consists of articles which are funds appropriated, and paid into the exchequer of the country (*i.e.*, the native) Government."[18]

With this inland trade, the East India Company, (a collective body of foreign merchants incorporated) had no direct concern.[19] The Company, with infinite pains and expense, had, by their agents

17. Verelst: *A View of the Rise and Progress of the British Government in Bengal.* Appendix p. 44.

18. Vansittart: *Original Papers* Vol. 1, p. XXVII.

19. Such as the firmand obtained by Hamilton 1716, and the treaty obtained by Surman. No new trade privileges had been acquired from Mir Jafar by Clive and Watson.

procured from the Mogul freedom from duties (except at the Port of Surat,) for all goods exported by and belonging to the *collective* body but the Company had never sought to obtain privileges for the *private* trade of their servants. For the goods which were to pass duty-free, under the privilege bestowed by the Mogul Government, it was customary for the Governor, or the chiefs of the several factories to grant *dustucks* or passports, but the grant of a dustuck to cover goods acquired by the Company's servants, not as *agents* of the Company, but as private merchants on their own account, would—or rather should—have been regarded as fraudulent. For as Vansittart very truly observes : "It never could be intended by the Mogul King that *private foreign* merchants should be upon a better footing than private native merchants. If any set of foreign merchants could deal in all goods produced in the country, and sold in any part of the same country, free from all duties (while at the same time all duties were paid by the natives), the foreigners must, in consequence, keep the whole trade to themselves, and also the Government of the country must lose the whole of the duties."

Simple and obvious as this distinction between the export trade of the Company and the private and inland trade of its individual servants is in itself, it was not one that the Company's servants cared either to draw or to remember when drawn for their edification. There was in the land an only too numerous class of English merchants devoid of scruple, as Hastings in April 1762 wrote :

> "The oppression committed under the sanction of the English name, and through want of spirit in the Nabob's subjects to oppose them......this evil, I am well assured is practised all over the country by people falsely assuming the habits of our sepoys or calling themselves our Gomastahs.......I have been surprised to meet with several English flags flying in places which I have passed, and on the river. I do not believe that I passed a boat without one. By whatever title they have been assumed (for I could only trust to the information of my eyes, without stopping to ask questions), I am sure their frequency can bode no good to the Nabob's revenues, the quiet of the country, or the honour of the nation, but evidently tend to lessen each of them.......You are sensible, Sir, that it is from such little irregularities, too trivial perhaps for publick complaint, and continually repeated, that the country people are habituated to entertain the most unfavourable notions of our government, and by them the English credit suffers much more, than by matters which are made of greater consequence in the debates between the Nabob and us."

It would be no difficult task to paint in lurid yet truthful colours a sad picture of Bengal in these circumstances : but we will be content with reproducing Vansittart's curt but forcible analysis :

> Private factors (gomastahs) set themselves up for judges of causes, particularly where their own interests are concerned, or that of their masters ; beating and binding officers of considerable station in the country government—soldiers and sepoys attending their orders—they forcibly took away goods, they dealt in all merchandize, fixed their own prices, extorted payment, hoisted English colours, forged passes, would give no account of themselves—shops were shut up—villages abandoned—and nothing was heard of but outcries on the one hand, against the tyranny and oppressions of the English and their gomastahs ; and on the other against the insolence of the Nawab and his officers."

In judging Ellis' transactions at Patna the facts we have recited have to be carefully borne in mind. For instance, the charge against Munseram, that he had "stopped some opium belonging to Mr. Hay, notwithstanding there was a *dustuck* with it, and will not let it pass." Here—I may be wrong—but I imagine an instance of Vansittart's wide statement "every struggle made by the country people against the oppression and extortion of *private* English gomastah's trade, was immediately construed as an attack upon the Company's rights."

7. SUMMARY.

Vansittart had commenced his rule by offending the majority of those who were to act with him in Council: thus it was possible for Carnac to close a letter, almost contemptuous in its terms with this passage: "Yet in this I am not singular, as I wisely believe, if the whole Board could be assembled (........., the half, if not the majority) would be found to concur with me in sentiment." The deposition of Mir Jafar, to which Holwell's excitable policy had led the way, had been a shock to the moral feeling of not a few of the Council and espicially to the officers of the Army; and to the latter the suspicion that Vansittart would betray Ramnarain, as he did betray him, into the hands of Mir Kasim, was an even greater trouble. As we read to-day the pages of Vansittart's books, we cannot help feeling that he to the end felt himself committed to an "impossible loyalty" in hoping against hope in the honesty and capacity of his creation—Mir Kasim. The story of the inland trade, however, is the heart of the whole matter. For it is clear that if the privileges which had been secured for the Company's export trade were to be held to cover the private and inland trade of the Company's servants, the result must have been not only the ruin of native merchants, trading on their own behalf, but of the native Government, which, on these terms, would sacrifice its revenue. In 1762, the prescient mind of Hastings had appreciated the fact that behind the trading difficulty lay a profound political problem: "Nothing, I fear," he wrote to Vansittart, "will reach the root of these evils, till some certain boundary be placed between the Nabob's authority and our privileges." When in 1765, Vansittart published his *Original Papers*, writing of the inland trade he said: "unless it be quite abolished, or wisely regulated, it must be the source of continual disputes. It can never be settled, unless the boundaries of the Company's jurisdiction and the country government's authority be fixed," and then he stated a dilemma.

1. If the Company could set up a title to, and could actually take possession of the whole province of Bengal, they could not garrison and protect it. If they do not take possession of the whole province and the government cannot have the fruits of its own duties and revenues, there will be perpetual sources of disputes.

2. Nor can any Mogul or Nawab, or the subjects of either, be contented with the residence of such guests; and the whole continent, for their own interests, will be ready to join against them.

The working out of this problem in logic, not logically stated, was facilitated by the violence of Mir Kasim.

8. THE MISSION OF WARREN HASTINGS TO MIR KASIM.

In view of the disputes between the Chief of Patna and the Nawab it was thought well that a person, in whom the Nawab had great confidence, should be sent to reassure him that the confidence placed in him by the Government was in no way relaxed. For this purpose no more suitable person could be found than Warren Hastings, who as a former factor at Cossimbazar and Resident at the Moradbag, was familiar with the ways of the Court of Murshidabad. The terms of the envoy's instructions were as follows:

March 15*th*, 1762.

We have observed, for some time past, an uneasiness or jealousy in the Nabob's conduct, which we can attribute to nothing but the false reports and representations of mischievous persons, and being desirous of convincing him, that we wish for nothing more than to preserve the present tranquility of the country, to avoid all disputes, and to conform to the terms of the treaty subsisting between him and the Company, we think proper to depute you, in whom the Nabob has great confidence, to make him these assurances on our behalf.

At the same time, we should be extremely glad to discover who have been the secret authors of this growing jealousy. We imagine, there may be some, as well as amongst the persons living under our protection, as about the Nabob's person. You may assure the Nabob that we shall severely punish those who belong to us, whenever we can fix the guilt, and you will strenuously recommend to him to do the same on his part.

The sooner you can set out on this commission the better, that the bad effects, which the want of confidence between us and the Nabob might occasion in the country may be prevented.

In these instructions there may perhaps be a threat on the Governor's part addressed to the opposition, but if threat there was, it was met by the opposition with a cruel piece of irony. I do not think that any writer has, before this, regarded the motion which Mr. Amyatt moved on "the next Council day but one" in its true character as a very cruel jest at the Governor's expense. Solemnly Amyatt arose in his place and moved:

"Mr. Amyatt recollects the President having mentioned that 20 lakhs of rupees were promised by Cossim Aly Cawn to the Board, but that he would not consent to this money being received till the debt to the Company was paid. As that is now satisfied, Mr. Amyatt is of opinion, it should be made a part of Mr. Hastings' instructions to endeavour to recover the promised 20 lakhs. and when recovered that instead of being distributed amongst the members of the Council, which could not fail of raising a suspicion that our assents to the Revolution were bought, the money should be placed to the credit of the Company." The persons who were to receive this refreshment were Vansittart, Holwell, Caillaud, Sumner and McGuire!

Solemnly Mr. Hay contended that the bond for twenty lakhs, having been returned by the Governor, without an order from the Board, had been returned without proper authority, and its payment must, therefore, be insisted upon: and Johnstone gave a similar opinion, adding however, that "the Company might have expected their agents to have accepted and transferred it to their account." Carnac put forward the paradox that only by insisting upon the payment could the Board justify itself, "for, however, innocent the gentlemen of the Board may be, they would probably imagine that they have all received some pecuniary consideration, in return for having appointed Cassim Allee Cawn to the *Subahdaree*, whereas from this demand being made the contrary will appear upon record."[20]

The President's reply was dignified and the facts he revealed do great honour to his integrity. Not only he, but Holwell, Sumner, and McGuire, had declined to receive Mir Kasim's offer of 20 lakhs. On the birth of his son, the Governor had received a bill for Rs. 25,000 from the Nawab, and this had been paid into the Company's treasury. Up to February 8th, 1762, the Nawab had paid six lakhs of sicca rupees to the Company, the Ceded Provinces had yielded 53 lakhs of current rupees.[21] With what pretence could more be asked? The demand now proposed could only increase the uneasiness which had been observed. "I hope," the Governor continued, "that such is not Amyatt's view in making this proposal; but it is hard to conceive from what motive it can have proceeded. Certainly, it is not from pure regard to the Company, nor from any conviction of the justness of the claim; for he never thought of offering the Company what he received of the Nawab Jaffar Allee Cawn's present to the Council and Committee; nor ever gave it as his opinion that the Company had a right to it."[22]

20. *Narrative*. Vol. II. p. 28.
21. The Sicca Rupee was worth 2s. 8½d.; the current 2s. 4d.
22. *Narrative*. Vol. II. pp. 34-35.

The majority, however, decided that the demand should be made, and instructions to that effect were added to Hastings' papers. On April the 9th, he set out. and arrived at Patna on May 2nd, where he had hoped to meet Ellis, but that gentleman had betaken himself to his country house at Singia, about 15 miles from the city, and was careful to remain there during the five days Hastings remained at Patna. Hastings then pushed on to meet the Nawab at Sassaram. The Nawab warmly repudiated any unfriendliness, or jealousy of the English on his part, and if any person in his following could be pointed out as guilty of fomenting disaffection, he would make an example of him. "It grieves me, that without cause or enquiry, you, Gentlemen, suffer such suspicions to take place in your hearts, and declare them to me, your friend. Who it is belonging to yourselves, that is continually speaking evil of me, propagating calumnies against me, and representing me to you as your enemy, is not unknown to you. The acts of violence committed by Mr. Ellis before my face; the insults on my people, and the disturbances raised in the country; my authority rendered contemplible to all Indostan; and obstructions thrown in the way of every business of the Government, in the province of Behar."[23]

The intractible character of Mr. Ellis seemed for the moment the one difficulty in the way of a perfect understanding with Mir Kasim—a difficulty made insurmountable by the fact that, as Hastings put it, "the most glaring misconduct in him (Ellis) would meet with support from a majority in the Board."[24] In the end Hastings' mission could produce nothing better than good advice to two absolutely irreconcilable foes.

---

9. VANSITTART'S ATTEMPT TO REGULATE THE INLAND TRADE.

It was this mission of Warren Hastings which brought into prominence the serious problem of the inland trade. While at Sasseram, Hastings explained to the Nawab the strict regulations, which the Governor wished to be adopted with a view to bring to an end the abuse of the English flag on country-laden boats. We are here concerned not with these regulations but with their consequences. The nature of the private inland trade has already been defined, but it has yet to be pointed out that while the private traders failed to see that the privileges secured for the Company's export trade could not cover their own private adventures without placing the native merchants at an enormous disadvantage, the Nawab, on the other hand, was ready to crush the inland trade of the European merchants out of all existence. Vansittart and Hastings were prepared to admit, and did admit, that the Imperial firmands gave no privileges of *dustuck* to private trade, and that therefore, the European merchants were bound to pay, as did the native, the customary duties; but the position maintained by the Nawab was that his predecessors had in times past restrained the European merchants from carrying on inland trade upon any footing whatsoever. The right to buy and sell country products within the country, he claimed, was entirely in his own hands, and he had watched with suspicion and disgust the new markets under English gamastahs which were springing into existence in even the most remote parts of his provinces. The Governor's contention is succinctly stated in a letter addressed to the Council from Monghyr by himself and Warren Hastings, December 15th, 1762:

> As on the one hand we do not see any reasons why the English gentlemen, and other inhabitants of Calcutta, and the subordinate factories, should carry on the inland trade with the Company's *dustuck*, or in any other respect, more advantageously than the country merchants, so, on the other hand, we think it would be a great hardship if, we and all belonging to us were not admitted upon an equality with the merchants

23. *Ibid.* p. 47.
24. *Ibid.* p. 61.

and inhabitants of other parts of Bengal, and suffered to trade on equal terms, in all commodities, and in all places, provided our agents and gomastahs do not set themselves up for magistrates in the country, and carry on their business by force and oppression.[25]

If then, on the one hand the English merchants were inclined to abuse the Company's privileges by covering their own private merchandise by a *dustuck* only lawfully applicable to sea-borne trade, the Nawab on the other evinced a strong inclination to impede their inland trade on any footing whatsoever. In these circumstances it cannot be doubted that the restrictions on the passage of boats on the river to which Hastings gave assent, on behalf of the Governor, on May 18th, 1762, must have given a handle to the always lawless and insolent officers of Mir Kasim, who could make these otherwise laudable measures a pretext for interfering with the inland trade, howsoever lawfully and peacefully conducted.

To return to the course of events, through which we must travel with greater speed, now that the essence of the existing troubles has been explained: In June, 1762, Hastings returned to Calcutta. For two months the Governor was laid up by a dangerous illness, and Amyatt presided in his room. "The first I heard of business after my recovery," he writes, "was that a war was breaking out with the Nawab, complaints crowded in upon me from all parts, the officers of the Government declaring that their authority was trampled upon by the English gomastahs, so that they could no longer preserve the least order, in the management of the business committed to their charge, nor collect the revenues of the Government, and that the usual duties which had been paid by the English merchants on salt and some other articles of trade were now withheld and refused; and, on the other side, the gentlemen of the subordinate factories and the English gomastahs, asserting that they had paid the usual duties, notwithstanding which many of their boats were stopped.[26]

Anxious both to obtain a change of air, and to see what could be effected by his immediate presence, Vansittart determined to pay the Nabob a visit at Monghyr, and accordingly, with Hastings as his assistant, he set out on October the 20th. He reached Murshidabad on the 3rd, and stayed there doing business till the 12th; on the 30th he arrived at Monghyr, "where the Nabob received me with all the usual marks of respect. Hardly a day past, but I went with Mr. Hastings to visit the Nabob, or he came to us. His constant topick was the ill-treatment he had received from Mr. Ellis, the injustice done him by me, the Council, in not resenting such proceedings. As I knew it was out of my power to give him any satisfaction in that point, I answered that all these disputes were long passed; and that now he and I were met together, such regulations should be made, as would be satisfactory to both parties, and prevent disputes in future. He was always warm upon this argument; and I found that he and Mr. Ellis could never be friends: however, I hoped, that the occasions of dispute might be removed, and their enmity lie burried within their own breasts."

Poor optimistic Vansittart! Within a year from this date Mir Kasim was to be the murderer of Ellis and Amyatt, and a crowd of unarmed unoffensive English prisoners. It has been said that the character of a Government may be judged by the nature of the opposition it provokes. When three years after the occurrence of the Patna massacres, Vansittart published his *Narrative*, he was clearly of opinion that his experiment with Mir Kasim had been the right policy, but it is not clear that he ever made any patient endeavour to understand the opposition which his support of the intruded Nabob provoked.

Vansittart tells us that the Nawab next complained "of the innovations in the private trade, as salt, beetle-nut, tobacco, etc., and the insolent authority usurped by our gomasthas

25. *Ibid.* p. 154.
26. *Ibid.* Vol. II, pp. 110-11.

employed in carrying it on in the distant parts of the country. He urged that we had no right to this trade from our firmann, that it occasioned incredible damage and disorder to his government, and this for the advantage only of particulars; and in short insisted that we should continue it no longer, but confine our private trade in the same manner it was before the government of Meer Jafar. Although I was of the same opinion with the Nabob, as to the rights of the firmann; that they could not be construed to extend further than the trade in articles imported by shipping, and the manufactures and products of the country for exportation, yet I was unwilling to give up an advantage, which had been enjoyed by the Company's servants in a greater or less degree for five or six years; and therefore told the Nabob, that as to the inland trade, or the trade from place to place in the country, we meant only to carry it on upon the same footing with other merchants; that we had always paid more or less duties to the government on this trade; but as the rates were not fixed and regulated, many disputes arose on that account; that we could inform ourselves of the rate of duties paid by the Moors and other merchants; and accordingly to that give a general order that duties should be paid in all parts. To this the Nabob consented with difficulty, and declared, that if after this regulation any more disputes should arise, and the duties agreed on should not be paid, he should have no remedy left, but laying all trade entirely open, and giving a general liberty to the merchants of the country, and all other nations, to carry on their commerce, custom free".

In due course, Vansittart and Hastings settled with the Nawab a treaty for the inland trade as follows :—

1st. That for all trade imported or exported by shipping, the Company's *dustuck* shall be granted, and it shall pass unmolested and free of custom as usual.

2nd. For all trade from one place in the country to another, in commodities produced in the country, as salt, beetle-nut, tobacco, etc., the Company's *dustuck* shall not be granted: but it shall go with the *dustuck* of the buxbunder, shahbunder, or other officer of the country government.

3rd. That at the time of taking out the said *dustuck*, and before the despatch of the goods, the duties shall be paid according to the rates, which shall be particularly settled and annexed to this agreement.

4th. That the said duties, so to be paid before the exportation, shall be the whole that are to be paid: so that after the despatch of the goods, nothing shall be paid at the chokeys in the road, nor at the place of sale.

5th. That all goods, being furnished either with the Company's *dustuck* or that of the government, shall meet with no obstruction or delay. The guards and chokeys on the road shall have nothing more to do than demand a sight of the *dustuck*, unless they shall observe the boats to be laden with a larger quantity of goods than are mentioned in the *dustuck*; in which case, they are to give immediate notice to the nearest English factory, as well as to the nearest officer of the government, that orders may be sent to have a strict examination; but they are not to detain them in the road.

6th. If any one should attempt to pass goods without a *dustuck*, either from the government or the company, or shall clandestinely forward a Company's *dustuck* to pass salt, tobacco, or other produce of the country from place to place, for inland trade, such goods shall be seized and confiscated. The guards and chokeys in the road are to stop them, and to give notice to the nearest English factory, as well as to the nearest officer of the government.

7th. If any person, not having a *dustuck*, shall attempt to pass boats, or goods clandestinely, under the care of, and in company with other boats or goods having a *dustuck*, such boats or goods so attempted to be passed clandestinely shall be seized and confiscated.

8th. The gomastahs in every place shall carry on their trade freely, and as merchants, and shall on no account use force in buying and selling. If any disputes arise in the course of their business, they shall not attempt to redress them themselves, but shall make their complaints to the Fouzedar, or other officer of the government, and have the matter tried before him. In like manner, if any merchant or inhabitant shall be aggrieved by any English gomastah, he shall make his complaints to the Fouzedar, or other officer of the government; and the gomastah being duly summoned, shall appear before him to answer to the charge, and have the matter determined.

9th. To deter the Fouzedars and other officers of the government from being guilty of any partiality, they shall be enjoined to transmit to the Nabob copies of their proceedings, upon all trials where English agents or gomasthas are concerned; likewise to give a copy to the agent or gomastah, who, if he thinks himself aggrieved, may send the same to his principal; and he may make his complaint to the President, who, if the case requires it, will apply to the Nabob for redress; and when any fouzedar, or other officer of the government, shall be proved guilty of such partiality, the Nabob shall punish him in the most exemplary manner."

These regulations, reasonable as they cannot but appear to us, were to become the subject of violent quarrels.

10. VANSITTART AND HASTINGS AT PATNA.

Having paid farewell to Mir Kasim, who was setting out with his army on an expedition against Betiah and Nepal, the Governor and his assistant left for Patna, which place they reached on January 1st, 1763. Four days were spent here in discussing with Ellis the complaints which the Nabob's deputy had to put forward, and which chiefly concerned the Burbunna gate—a small wicket in the N. W. quarter of the city, and a *ganj* known as *Colonelganj*, which had been set up "without any right, grant or order, either from the Company or the Nabob." The point about the gate was that it afforded a short cut into the city for the folk at the factory, who would have otherwise had to go five or six hundred yards round to the west gate of the city; but the Nabob insisted that, in the interest of good order in the city, the wicket must be closed, and the Governor thought it best to comply. Orders were given that *Colonelganj* should be abolished. The Governor left Patna on January 5th, and Monghyr on the 9th. On January 16th he left Cassimbazar, "upon hearing news of the French ships in Balesore Road, and arrived in Calcutta on the 18th."

11. THE CONFLICT IN THE COUNCIL.

And now it was Vansittart's turn to have some experience of the difficulty of dealing with Mir Kasim. At Monghyr the Governor had explained to the Nabob that *upon his arrival at Calcutta*, orders from *the Board* would be sent, in consequence of the regulations agreed upon, to all the subordinate factories: the Nabob knew well that the Governor's orders could not take effect till joined with those of the Board, which last he himself had asked for: but, writes

Vansittart, "I had hardly left him when he despatched copies of my letters to his officers in all parts of the country, with general orders for their observance; and a direction that all English gomastahs, who refused to comply with them, should be turned out of the country."

This act of suicidal folly on the part of the Nabob can only be explained on the supposition that he had bitterly repented of the concession allowed English merchants to carry on their private trade on equal terms with the native merchants. He had no doubt formed the opinion that Vansittart was a man of weak character, and so much committed to supporting his, (the Nabob's) interests, that, armed with the authority of the Governor's letters, he would be in a fair way of being able to route out the English trade and traders piece-meal. As Mir Kasim's action was so well calculated to drive the Governor to side with his opponent at the Council, it may with safety be said that the Nabob, by this step, embarked on that course of recklessness which was to end in measures which nothing could ever atone for and which could only gratify a lust for revenge. To add folly to folly, the Nabob, in one of his letters, exempted the private trade of Vansittart and Hastings from liability.

The Governor now found himself in an absolutely impossible situation, and the more so because he had, while at Monghyr, received £50,000 promised to himself, and £20,000 for Colonel Caillaud. "He was ill-fitted by nature," writes Elphinstone, "to bear up against the reckless counsels and vehement language of his opponents, and he was rendered feebler than usual by the consciousness of his pecuniary obligations to the Nabob, and by his being himself engaged in the inland trade, though without taking in the abuses."[27] On his arrival at Calcutta he learned from Amyatt that orders had been sent for all the members of the Board to come down from the subordinate settlements, with the exception of the Chiefs of Patna and Chittagong (on account of the distances) and that Major Carnac had taken his seat. On February 1st the Governor entered a lengthy minute[28] on the consultations in which he defended his transactions in the matter of the regulation of the inland trade, and in particular made reply to the factors at Dacca who had in vigorous terms represented the loss in which the new regulations would involve their concerns. He stooped to deal with an insinuation conveyed in a letter from Johnstone and Hay to the effect that the motive of the restraint placed on the trade of others was the advancement of his own private affairs. "As to the Major, he is a member of the Board, according to our Hon'ble Masters directions, *when military matters only are under debate.* How the regulation of a method for carrying on our trade in salt, beetle-nut, and tobacco, can be brought under that title I cannot conceive, nor how he can be supposed to be a Judge of such a subject; yet if you conceive his advice can be of use, I am far from objecting to his being present." In the meanwhile, pending the assembling of the full Council, the Governor wrote to the Nawab that other regulations would be made by the Council and that he must restrain his people from exercising acts of violence against the English agent. Amyatt, who had presided at the Board during Vansittart's absence, also delivered a minute denying that any authority had been conferred on the President for the enterprising of the late transactions.

On February 15th the Council met, including Vansittart, Amyatt, Batson (Chief of Kasimbazar), Billiers (Chief of Luckypore), Cartier (Chief of Dacca), Hastings, Johnstone (Chief of Burdwan), Hay, Marriott and Watts. To the motion that Carnac should be called in, all agreed, save the President, Hastings and Watts, and as the majority were in favour of Carnac being called, Major Adams also took his seat. The proceedings commenced with a minute presented by Amyatt

27 *Ibid.* p. 144. Elphinstone: *The Rise of the British Power in the East* p. 383.
28. *Narrative*: Vol. II, pp. 234-253.

in which the whole proceedings of the Governor at Monghyr and Patna were censured.[29] Before the proceedings for the day closed, Carnac delivered a letter claiming the command at Patna—"the station of Patna being the most likely quarter from whence we may expect troubles"—a claim which Vansittart opined had "all the appearance of his wishing to make them (the disputes with the Nawab) worse, and to be more at hand to act in concert with Mr. Ellis to that end."

On the consultations of February 18th and 19th, when the Nawab's demand in regard to the Babunna gate was dealt with, we find not one member of the Council defended the Governor's decision, while two or three assigned to the Nawab an intent to offer an indignity to the English nation and possibly an act of hostility. In consequence a letter in peremptory terms was written to the Nabob calling on him to re-open the gate. In the matter of the ganj, the Council unanimously supported the Governor.

If we were engaged on a general history of the English in Bengal and not simply with the humbler task of sketching the events which led up to the massacres at Patna, it would be necessary to give here a detailed account of the transactions of the Council from day to day, and nothing indeed would be found more interesting than a comparison of the views maintained in the several minutes ; but we must hasten our pace. It was agreed that the Governor had in his letter exceeded his powers—"a decision", writes Elphinstone, "which if it had not been accompanied with violence and invective, would have been justified by the fact."[30] With the exception of Vansittart and Hastings, all held that the imperial firmands entitled them to trade in country produce duty-free, although seven of the twelve thought that, of favour but not of right, the Nawab should be allowed a duty of two and a half per cent. on salt ; the Governor had agreed with the Nawab for nine. To a resolution, which, as Elphinstone tersely puts it, determined that "the agents were to be the only judges in all their disputes with private persons, and the chief of the factory in those with the Nawab's defendants" even Vansittart agreed, Hastings alone dissenting ; and in these troubled days of ours, the words of the strenuous ruler of later days, are worth recalling :—"As I have formerly lived among the country people in a very inferior station, and at a time when we were subject to the most slavish dependence on the Government, and have met with the greatest indulgence, and even respect, from zemindars and officers of Government, I can with the greater confidence deny the justice of this opinion ; I add further from repeated experience, that if our people, instead of erecting themselves into lords and oppressors of the country, confine themselves to an honest and fair trade, they will everywhere be courted and esteemed."

12. THE GROWING FURY OF THE NAWAB.

We parted last with Mir Kasim as he was setting forth on his expedition against Nepal. If the account in the *Seir-i-Mutaqherin* is to be credited, the conduct of this expedition was calculated to cover the Nawab with disgrace, and to justify the opinion which Carnac had long ago expressed as to his cowardice. It could have been in no cheerful mood that the Nawab returned from Betiah to face once more his problem with the English. The first thing he was made to appreciate was that he had been dealing not with a Clive but a Vansittart. His letter of the 22nd of February may be taken truly indicating his feelings ; he had imagined that the Governor's word to be law.

29. "Whoever", writes Vansittart, "has read the former part of this narrative will easily perceive the distinguishing characteristics of Major Carnac's style throughout this writing delivered in by Mr. Amyatt." Elphinstone (*op. cit* p. 383) writes: "It is true that Major Carnac corresponded with Mr. Ellis, in cipher, and was the centre of all the correspondence of the malcontents throughout the civil service. but it does not appear that he and Mr. Ellis had any plan for bringing on a rupture, though like all the rest of their party they looked to it with pleasure."

30. *Op. Cit.* p. 335.

When you came here, an agreement in writing was made between us, which I imagined all the gentlemen would consent to; but it is amazing that not a single person has approved of it. Notwithstanding all you have expressly directed to the chiefs at Patna and Dacca factories, they do not pay any regard to it, but return for answer: "We do not approve of the Governor's proceedings; when the gentlemen of the Council write to us, we will immediately follow their directions."

Since the commencement of Meer Mahamed Jaffer Cawn's management to the present time, I have not known any one but yourself.[31] Now the gentlemen of all the factories do not regard your directions, but require the orders of the Council, and they ruin the affairs of both this province [Behar] and Bengal, the zemindarees, the merchandise, the riats, etc., for what reason I cannot conceive. I neither have, nor shall negotiate with any person but yourself; and therefore I plainly write, that if you intend to regard the agreement made between us, you should act in such a manner that the gentlemen may not make their objections to it; if not, advise me of it. I understand that a number of the gentlemen are inclined to establish another Subahdar. This appears to me a trivial matter. Let them establish whom they please; it is of no consequence to me. I do not regard matters of so small importance. God made the world, and everything is made by Him........................I gave you lands to the amount of fifty lacks of rupees, for the maintenance of troops to destroy my enemies; but it is amazing that a number of gentlemen have, on the contrary, collected troops against me in order to ruin my country. It is the universal persuasion that Europeans are to be confided in; but to see all this surprises me.

In a letter dated, February the 26th the Nawab is even still more effective. Is it too much to be hoped that some day it will be practicable for the Calcutta Historical Society or the Asiatic Society of Bengal, to publish a volume of Mir Kasim's letters, the Persian text on one page, and the translation facing it? This letter concludes.

As to what you write of my officers, it appears from thence that the agreement made between us, the Council has not assented to. To be sure, whatever *your* gomastahs write, is all exactly just and proper, and *my* people tell nothing but lies and barefaced falsities. I must have all losses in your trade made good to you; but who will indemnify me for the loss of revenues, partly due to my government?

I must cut off my officers' heads, but your gomastahs, who are guilty of oppressions, receive encouragement from you. You know very well, Sir, that I never intended such a treaty; it was merely in compliance with your pleasure that I assented to it. Now that the Council do not agree to it, and want to make another treaty, this is unreasonable. These demands, which I formerly made to you, I now again repeat. The first is this: from the beginning till now, the Nazim of Bengal corresponded with the Governor of Calcutta, as I have done and do with you, having no correspondence with the rest of the Board.

The second is, I have before remarked to you, that the Company's trade has been established from time immemorial; but, at present, besides the Company's trade, the gomastahs of the English gentlemen have set up the trade of salt, tobacco, dried fish, timbers, etc., and purchase from the country people by force, and extortion, and are continually making unjust disputes and wrangling with my officers; so that the poor, the inhabitants,

31. *Narrative*. Vol. 41. pp. 6-8 By "you", "yourself" in this letter, I take it that Mir Kasim means the Governor *ex officio*, and not Vansittart exclusively, for Vansittart was not in Bengal when Mir Jafar was placed on the *musnud*.

the merchants, and manufacturers of my country are oppressed, and both you and myself are troubled with unjust vexations. Now, I say, that your gomastahs are to trade as heretofore, in merchandize imported and exported; and are to refrain from those articles of trade which interfere with the revenues due to my government and are a cause of disputes, and the ruin of the inhabitants and poor people.

The third is whether I shall have the charge of the expense of the army, and management of the country, and his Majesty's revenues; and that your gomastahs shall carry on those branches of trade, which were never allowed in the country, by interfering in the government, under the pretence of trade, and that my officers shall not have their authority, nor offer to oppose them. If this be the case, it is out of my power to carry on the business of this subahdaree. I wish not to be concerned in a charge of so much vexation; you may be pleased to find some other to undertake it. For my part I am heartily tired of these disputes and vexations. Why do you take the trouble to send forces against my officers? Why do you write to them to quit their stations; and repair to me, for they have no forces to oppose you? You are sensible that in Chittagong, Midnapore, and Burdwan, which, agreeable to treaty, I ceded to the Company, not a man of mine ever enters, and I refrain even from providing the customary cloths for my own use. If you do not determine justly for me, it is a matter of great surprise.

Mir Kasim's professed ignorance of the powers of the Board, had, of course, the effect of making the members of that body very anxious to enlighten him and that in a manner very ill calculated to protect the dignity of the Governor. It was determined that a passage should be added to the letter addressed by the Governor to the Nawab explaining that the former was only their agent, and that the decision of matters lay with the majority of the Council. Hay, indeed would have gone further, and actually moved that a letter should be written by the whole Board, but his motion was lost. It now, however, seemed clear to all that the disputes had gone so far, that to avert a final rupture and war, a peaceful negotiation carried on by representatives of the majority on the Council must be tried. For this purpose Amyatt and Hay were selected as envoys, but before the Nawab's consent to this mission had been obtained, acts of violence of an even more marked character had been perpetrated. From Dacca came the news of a fray between the native officers and a party of sepoys who had been sent to release some boats detained at Jafarganj; and it might well have been expected that incidents of the kind would become of daily occurrence, so long as the Nawab's people on the one hand were under orders to act under the Governor's letter, and the factors, on the other, were enjoined by the Board to resist by force any interference. On the very day this intelligence arrived from Dacca, the news came of a far more serious disturbance in Behar. Lieutenant Dowrie had been despatched, at the head of three companies of seepoys to Mow, with instructions to "clear the Company's business" and "to seize all who have interrupted it." The Lieutenant captured Akbar Ali Khan, the Nabab's collector, and brought him prisoner to Patna having left a company of sepoys at Taagepore, to keep guard over the Company's saltpetre. Mir Kasim had ordered a body of 500 horsemen to intercept the detachment, but arriving too late on the scene, they made for Taagepore, and after hard fighting captured the Company's sepoys and the gomastah. The Nawab, who still evinced hesitation in proceding to extremities, having reprimanded the gomastah, ordered the captives to be released.

During the month of March, Mir Kasim sent a succession of letters to the Governor showing how great was his irritation, and naming Ellis as the author of all this violence and his bitter unrelenting foe. "If you are inclined to allow of Mr. Ellis' action, you will do well to give the country to him, that you and I may be freed from the vexations of it; for I am convinced that the Council will not put an end to these disputes. Certainly, the Council had no such intention, at least not until their trade had been secured. In one letter Mir Kasim goes so far as to employ the phrase "your servants and men of low character;" in another, he writes "I have no resource, but to make use, as you do, of expressions tending to dissolve our friendship." These letters were read in Council on March 24th, and the Governor was called upon to address a reply to the Nawab which may perhaps be styled an ultimatum.

> I have received your letters of the 11th, 14th and 15th instant. With regard to the interruptions of our trade, and the disputes, which have happened between the dependents of your Government and ours, our original orders were to apply to you and your officers for redress, on any occasion of complaint on our part; but this was so often done without effect that, finding the interruptions and disturbances daily increase, insomuch that our business was in most parts put an entire stop to, we had no remedy left to make use of, but that of force, to free our business; and therefore, disagreeable as it was to us, we were obliged to give such orders to all the factories, of which you have been before duly advised.
>
> What Mr. Ellis has done in the Patna Province, for clearing the Company's business, was agreeable to the said orders, sent to him by the Board; and I must here particularly observe, with reference to that gentleman's not applying to you for redress on any occasion, that you have absolutely put it out of his power, by declaring that you would not answer any of his letters, and having really left unanswered four, which he actually wrote you.
>
> I do not find that you have yet given orders to any of your officers to forbare from obstructing our business, as they still continue to do it to the utmost of their power, excepting in those places where our troops are actually stationed for its protection; and when you have given such orders as shall put an end to these obstructions, we, on our part, will not interfere with your officers, or the officers of your government.
>
> I have wrote you before of our resolution and demands, and now I again acquaint you that we shall insist upon a compliance with them in every point. Myself, as well as the Council, are resolved to support you in your government and all its rights; but if you oppose our people in the execution of the orders, which we have authorized, and with which you have been acquainted, we shall look upon such conduct as an open declaration of war; but to show you our earnest desire to prevent such an event, we continue in our resolution to send you Mr. Amyatt (who will be accompanied by Mr. Hay) for the purpose we have before wrote you, as soon as we shall receive your answer to that letter.
>
> I must in this letter take notice of two particular phrases that you make use of, *servants and men of low character*. I am very unwilling to suppose you could by such unbecoming expressions, mean the gentlemen of Council; but they, with me, insist upon an explanation, as we will by no means suffer ourselves to be treated with disrespect.

Before this letter had been despatched, tidings reached Calcutta that Mir Kasim had executed a *coup d'etat*, the possibility of which he had more than hinted to Vansittart and Hastings at the time of their stay at Monghyr. The measure was as clever in itself, but as futile, from the statesman's point of view, as was that remarkably clever move—King James IInd's Declaration of Indulgence. Mir Kasim has evidently stolen that page from the *Arabian Nights* in which we read how a faithful lady instead, of wiping off the chalk on her master's door, chalked all the other doors. Called upon to remit the duties on English inland trade, Mir Kasim now remitted all duties for European and Native alike, for the space of two years. The effect of this intelligence on the Council has been thus described by Elphinstone.

> "This intelligence transported the ruling part of the Council beyond all bounds of reason. All declared it a violation of the Company's rights; some pronounced it an act of usurpation to remit the Emperor's customs without his leave, though they had themselves accepted both exemption and territories as little sanctioned by the Emperor; others denied the right of a Nabab whom they had raised to the Subahdarship and supported by force of arms against the King, to employ the power, with which they had been pleased to invest him to undermine their royal privileges and ruin their trade; and one member derided the notion of the Nawab's possessing any independence in his own territory, and treated the assertion of such a right as more worthy of his hired agents than of members of that board...........This was the tone adopted by men, who, seven years before, had lived in slavish dependence on the Nawab's government, and who, by their subsequent treaties had acquired no right or pretence for interfering in his internal administration. The motives they affected were proportioned to the greatness of their pretensions. No one hinted at the danger to their illicit gains; it was the honour of the factory, the dignity of the dustuck, above all, the glory of the nation, which was to suffer by the suppression of smuggling."[32]

Shortly after this meeting of Council, news came of tidings of violence, at the Nawab's instigation, at Gya, and also that his Deputy at Dacca had put a complete stop to the trade in that district. We cannot but be wondered why the Council did not at once direct that the army should in be readiness to march, for the measures which they decided should be taken were calculated to provoke a final rupture of their relations with Mir Kasim: and the Nawab, so far from welcoming the idea of the mission of Amyatt and Hay, was inclined to regard it as but a repetition of the mission which had deposed his predecessor. This view was expressed by Batson on April 1st, but the Governor still clung to the opinion that "the Nabob has not the design of breaking with us," and it was agreed that "the Nabob should again be wrote to, to insist of his receiving the deputation; and that Messrs. Amyatt and Hay should proceed to, and wait for his answer at Cossimbazar." A refusal on the Nawab's part to accept the demands of the Commission was to be held "a declaration on his side of his intention to come to a rupture with us."

13. THE DEPUTATION OF AMYATT AND HAY.

On April 9th, Amyatt and Hay took leave of the Board, departing with instructions, of which the Governor himself disapproved, but signed, as it was "the established rule of all the Company's Governments...that every member shall sign the public orders and records, entering his dissent, where he differs from the opinion of the majority in the consultations." For the terms of these instructions the reader is referred to Vansittart's *Original Papers Relative to the Disturbances in Bengal.* (Vol. 11, page 16 *et seq.*): it is unnecessary to reprint them here.

On the 15th the Nawab wrote "as to Mr. Amyatt's coming, which you wrote about before, I have no objection. Recall all your troops that you have despatched towards this way, and let Mr. Amyatt proceed hither in the same manner that you came to visit me and after his arrival I will behave to him as becomes me." But the very day before this letter was written, although the Nawab's idea that "forces in several divisions, with guns and artillery were already moving up through the hills and woods" was a delusion, the Board had adopted the military measures

32. Elphinstone *Op. Cit.* pages 389—90. The debate at the Council will be found in the third volume of Vansittart's *Narrative.* With all due deference, I cannot help thinking that, in as much as Mir Kasim's declarations of free trade would have been prejudical if not ruinous to the unquestioned privileges of the Company, and in as much that even free trade for the European merchant had been objected to by the Nawab, Elphinstone's sarcasm about the "suppression of smuggling" is effective but not wholly just.

which were to be taken should the rupture take place. If the Nawab were to march upon Patna, the English at that place were to endeavour to possess themselves of the city, and wait further orders from either the Council or Major Adams. Should the task of attacking the city seem too hazardous, then they must "take such post as they can best defend themselves in, and, if they can, cover the factory until they shall receive further orders as above mentioned. Should the Nawab remain at Monghyr they must follow the same course. Should he march on Calcutta, then, after having seized the city, they must move down to Ruinulla, to be in greater readiness to join Major Adams. The question was then raised: "How shall they be informed of a rupture, or what shall they construe as such." The difficulty lay, on the one hand, in the great distance between Patna and Calcutta and the consequent difficulty of keeping Ellis informed of what was going on, and, on the other, the possibility that the gentlemen at Patna, if left to take action at their own discretion, might by error involve the Company in a war. For safety's sake it was determined that the folk at the Patna factory should write for information from the Council before acting upon the plan laid down. To this, on the 9th of May, the Chief and Council at Patna made reply:

> We have received your favour of the 14th instant, with the resolutions of the Board, which, as far as we comprehend them, will not allow us to construe any act of the Nabob as hostile, although ever so greatly tending to our ruin: but we are to wait until we have notice from you of a rupture being declared. Who there may be to receive your commands, is hard to say, but most probably neither any of us, nor of the party now here, as we shall clearly evince.
>
> We had intelligence (not from hircarahs) that if the army should come from Calcutta, the Nabob intends marching here to attack us, in which case he will certainly remove our dauks,[33] and cut off all communication by that channel. It will be the third day of his march before we can receive certain advice of it, and a single cossid[34] will be twelve days reaching Calcutta, provded he meets with no impediment; but it is more probable that at such a juncture he never gets there, and still more so that your answer never reaches us. How, then, are we to act?
>
> This factory, it is well known, is not tenable, if attacked from the city, and to abandon it will, amongst other evils, give such a shock to the spirit of our troops as may induce the greatest part of our sepoys (in whom our principal strength consists) to desert us and go to the Nabob, where they are better insured of success, and will meet with ample encouragement, which has not been spared, even when there was no appearance of a rupture, to those who would desert with their arms. Another substantial reason why we cannot leave the factory is, our having put our ammunition, for its greater security, in the lower part of the house. The magazine, where it before lay, being liable to be blown up by a common rocket.
>
> But let us suppose for a moment that, on the Nabob's marching against us, we quit the factory, and take post. Are we to sacrifice our surgeons and sick who reside in the city? For it cannot be supposed that they will be permitted to come out, or if they could, the situation of most of them is such that their being brought into the air will be attended with certain death. When we have fortified ourselves in this post, our affairs are not all mended, for the Nawab has only to surround and starve us; whilst we, dying by inches, sit waiting for your orders, which can never arrive but with the army, which at the soonest will be forty days after its march from Monghyr. How are we to subsist all this time? The Nabab seizes all provisions coming from Bengal, and such is the scarcity here, that had it not been for the gung, which so much pains

33 Dauk (Dâk)—stationed letter-carriers.

34. *Original Papers*, Vol. II, pp. 202—4. Naib—a deputy: in this case the Nawab's Deputy.

was taken to abolish, we had long ere now been obliged to take up arms to procure our daily sustenance. But was there plenty, we have not a rupee to purchase it. With the utmost difficulty we have scraped money together to pay our troops for these two months past, and at this time have not sufficient to discharge a fourth part of the demands that will be upon us in a few days, although we acquainted you of the lowness of our cash as long ago as the 2nd of February.

This part, 'tis true, runs no risk from the Nabob, provided we are allowed to act, and make the most of every advantage that may offer ; but if our hands are tied, our destruction becomes inevitable. Such a body as this must ever act offensivly and vigorously, and nip the designs of the enemy in the bud. 'Tis by such conduct only that they can hope to preserve themselves, and surely it is just and laudable to make use of every means Providence has put in our power to defeat the attacks of a cruel and faithless enemy.

Our safety lies in mastering the city by a *coup de main* before the Nabob gets into it, for afterwards it may be impracticable, and the consequence of our acting on the defensive anywhere but in the city, we have already pointed out. Our distance from Calcutta is very great, and whenever the Nabob marches this way, our communication will be cut off, and most probably not opened but by your army. If, therefore, we should obey nature's first law, we hope we shall not be found culpable, though it may not perfectly coincide with your orders.

We cannot conclude without observing to you that we think we have noways merited the diffidence you express, nor given the least reason even to suspect that we would involve the Company in a war, by a rash and unprecedented step. We rather think that we have given proof of a contrary disposition in bearing the many insults we have received, particularly since Mindy Aly Caun has been appointed Naib here, whose people have even dared to allow and call us opprobrious names aloud from the walls.".............................

Before Amyatt and Hay could secure an interview, the Nawab had sent his officers to capture the two Jagat Sett brothers, Mahtab Rai and Raja Surup Chand, the heads of that great banking house, which had played so important a part in the history of Bengal since the first Revolution. To the protest which the English presented against this act, Mir Kasim replied contemptuously that when the English seize and carry away his officers no harm was held to be done, but if he should chance to summon a man, one of his own dependents, the treaty, of course, is violated. The Setts, so far from being mere men of commerce, had, he contended, mixed in every political intrigue : "they paid not the least regard to his summons, have put a stop to all their mercantile business, and have done all they could to throw the officers of the Nizamut into confusion," "and treating me as an enemy and outlaw."[35] He had brought them to Monghyr "with no other design than for the currency of business." In fact, as the author of the *Seir-i-Mutaqherin* tells us, Mir Kasim received the brethren with distinction, spoke to them with kindness, deplored the necessity of his affairs, soothed their minds, excused the rigour of his proceedings, and requested their living at Monghyr where he hoped they would build lodgings for themselves, set up a banking house, as they had at Murshidabad, attend at his court as they did formerly, transact business in the affairs of Government and finance. He, at the same time, set them at full liberty ; but people were secretly set upon them, with orders not to suffer them to go out any great distance. It only needs to be added here that, after his defeat at Udwanala, Mir Kasim, on his way from Monghyr to Patna, halted at Barr, he ordered the Setts to be murdered. According to the *Seír-i-Mutaqherin* they were hacked to pieces ; but according to local tradition they were drowned in the river.

35. *Ibid.* p. 504. The author, Seid Gholam Hossein Khan, a *protégé* of Mir Kasim, was present with the Nawab, throughout this period, and he gives a very interesting account of the transactions and conduct of Amyatt and his followers at the Nawab's Court.

On May 15th, Amyatt and Hay waited on the Nawab at Monghyr. At first there seemed to be some hope that the Nawab would accept the demands of the Company, but on either side there were complaints of a too haughty bearing. To throw everything into confusion, at this critical moment, some boats laden with arms for the English troops at Patna, which had been despatched two months before, in passing by Monghyr, were stopped by the Nawab's guards. This circumstance either served to cause a genuine allarm or else to afford a pretext for the claim, which Mir Kasim made at once, that the forces must be either brought down from Patna, or else Ellis must be recalled, and either Amyatt, McGuire, or Hastings appointed in his room.

Having received a number of letters from both Mir Kasim and the Deputation, a general Council, in June 9th, resolved that the troops should not be removed from Patna, and that if the Nabob persisted to demand it, or to detain the boats of arms, Messrs. Amyatt and Hay should be directed to leave Monghyr. At the same time the gentlemen at Patna were advised of these resolutions, and ordered to act as might be directed by Messrs. Amyatt and Hay.

The following is the account given by the author of the *Seir-i-Mutaqherin* of Amyatt's ill fated deputation :—

"Intelligence coming at this time that Mr. Amyatt was drawing near, the Navvab, who had beforehand sent for Mir-abdollah-sefevi from Azim-abad, a valuable gentleman, whose merit has many times been mentioned in these memoirs, now thought proper to join me, the poor man, to him in the same commission ; and he desired us, as we were both upon familiar terms with Mr. Amyatt, to go forward in order to receive him, and to endeavour to discover what was his real purpose. and what might be his real intentions in coming so far. He at the same time appointed a Gentoo, to attend us as Persian secretary, and he ordered twenty spies to be at our command both as spies and as messengers. These twenty men were parted in two divisions, and commanded by two head men as officers, who had orders to disguise themselves like menial servants, and to introduce themselves the one into Mir-abdollah's service, the other into mine, with injunctions never to be absent from any of the meetings or conferences which might be held with the English, and to take care to observe not only the expressions and words, but even the gestures of the hands as well as the head between us, transmitting every day a faithful account of what they should hear, or see. One of these twenty messengers, on receiving a letter, was to carry it to the next post, and then to return to his office. Every one of us having received our lesson in this manner, we quitted Monghyr, and arrived at Ganga-persad, where we had the good luck to meet Mr. Amyatt ; but on embracing him took care to whisper that we had spies over us. Mr. Amyatt and the others being thereby put upon their guard, spoke and acted with precaution ; for, being every night at the same landing place, we used to pass the greatest part of our time with the English ; and whatever we had said or heard, was fully set down both by us and by the head spies, and severally dispatched to the Navvab every evening. One day, to avoid all suspicions, I opened my commission to Mr. Amyatt with an audible voice, and I spoke to him as I had been instructed to do by the Navvab. "What can possibly be," said I, "the reason of your coming, and what is your intent? Being both of us well-wishers to His "Highness, as well as to the English, we are desirous of being informed of your intentions, that "we may contrive expedients for the benefit of both parties." Mr. Amyatt, with a loud voice, answered : "It is customary with Indians, when they come to us, to tell us none but such things "as may keep us in good humour ; and when they return to the Navvab, they never fail to speak "to him, so as to humour him in his wishes ; and hence our real intentions on both sides remain "concealed from each other party, and our views do not come to light. It is to avoid those "inconveniences, that we have quitted our homes, to come so far in embassy, with intention to see "the Navvab face to face, and to tell him what we have to say, as well as to hear what he has to "answer; and, this being the case, it is needless that we should have any business with any other "person." This declaration of Mr. Amyatt's putting an end to all political topics, we took care in our conversation with the English to drop many expressions of reproach, and to dispute with them in such a manner, as was pointed out by the times; it being the only expedient we could devise, to preserve ourselves from the Navvab's suspicions, and to avoid feeling the effects of his resentment. On the day when this last conversation took place, the contents of which were severally forwarded to Court both by us and by the head spies, we arrived at Baghalpoor and there received a letter from the Navvab, which recalled both Mir-abdollah and me, adding, that as Mr. Amyatt did not choose to enter into any particulars with us it was needless we should stay with him any more, but, that we must manage so as to be at Court before the Englishman's arrival. Mir-abdollah, having informed Mr. Amyatt of this recall, we took our leave of him, and returned to Monghyr, where we waited on the Navvab immediately, after having been met in the way by several messengers that came to hasten our march. Being in his presence, he commenced putting questions to us. As my poor friend, Mir-abdollah, (on whom be peace!) had not a ready delivery, and could not express himself properly, his answers displeased the Navvab, and he was twice reproached, and afterwards dismissed. He went home, and I followed him, with intent to take some rest; when a messenger came from Aaly-hibrahim-qhan, informing me that His Highness wanted me immediately, and that I must go with the Qhan to Court. Fain I was to put on a full dress again, and to repair to the Navvab's. This Prince was in his private apartments, sitting in the outer room of his bath, and in close conference with Ghurghin-qhan. I took my seat in a corner, and Aaly-hibrahim in another. The Navvab repeated to Gurghin-qhan what he had heard from my mouth; he then turned towards me, and ordering me to draw nearer, he bid me tell Gurghin-qhahn all my observations. Upon this command, I drew near, and sitting over against that General, I recommenced my tale. The General, after hearing a few words, seemed ruffled; and, to shew that my report deserved but little credit, he turned towards the Navvab, and said: *My Lord Navvab, were a man to rip open an Englishman's body with a knife, he would not for that come at his secret.* He then turned again to me. and asked me some questions, which I answered. At the third or fourth answer, he seemed impatient, and said: "My Lord Qhan, I want nothing of all that. Pray, do answer three or four questions which I am going to put to you. What is Mr. Amyatt's intention? And does he come to "intrigue against the Navvab, or not? Is he come to pry into the state of the army and fortress, "or not? Has he any friendship or good will for us, or does he come with hostile intention?" On hearing these words, I was extremely surprised, and looking at him full in the face, I answered: "My Lord, your questions really confound me, and I am amazed at what you mean. It is but a "moment since you said yourself, that were one to rip open an Englishman's body, he would not "for that come at his secret; and you want me now to reveal to you Mr. Amyatt's innermost "thoughts! As to his coming with sinister intentions, it would be really surprising that he should "harbour any such designs; the man comes into your house, and alone; and it is he that ought to "be afraid of sinister designs, and not you, who are at home, and ought not to conceive any fears "from him. As to what you have hinted of his coming hither to pry into the state of the army "and fortress, I am of opinion, that not only Mr. Amyatt shall, but that any other man whatever "that comes hither, will, of course, acquire some knowledge of both your fortress and your army; "and that the quantum of such a knowledge of his will depend on his share of penetration and "knowledge. With respect to your other two questions, about his coming with friendly or inimical "intentions, the matter of fact is, that he comes to you with some demands and requests of his "own; if you grant him his demands, there is no doubt but that he shall be pleased with you, and "will become your friend; and if you refuse them, it is no less certain that the refusal will produce "discontents,, and at last enmities. All these observations do not deserve questions; they are "self-evident." The Navvab having assented to what I said, Gurghin-qhan, who had never been a friend to me, became now more estranged than ever. But the Navvab dismissed me; and as I was going home in the utmost amazement, I could not but admire that fulness of power in the divine dispensations of Providence, which had suscited such and the like people, to stand over our heads as Generals of armies, and as Ministers of State, with unlimited powers of binding and loosing. The next morning after this conference, the Navvab sent his own nephew, Aabo-aaly-qhan, and his Minister Radja Nobet-ray, to meet and receive Mr. Amyatt; and on the third day, the latter arrived at Mongbyr, where he alighted at a set of tents that had been pitched up for his quarters. The Navvab went to see him, at which time the visit became one continued scene of dissimulation and reciprocal fringing. The next day Mr. Amyatt returned the visit. He had with him Mr. Hay, and Captain Johnston, together with some other gentlemen, amongst whom was a Mr. Gulston, a young man lately come into India, who in so short a time had learned the Persian very well, and at our first interview, had conceived as much good will for me as I had for him.[36] The Navvab, on descrying Mr. Amyatt, got up, as is the etiquette, advanced a few steps from his Mesned, and brought him to sit upon some chairs placed there on purpose, upon one of which he took his own seat. After a little conversation, the usual ceremonial of Paan, Atur, and Rose-water, was brought up; and then several trays covered with stuffs were produced, together with one plate containing jewels and gems; all which were presented to him. On his taking leave, the Navvab got up, and re-conducted him, as well as all the English, as far as the end of the carpeting, where he invited them to an entertainment. At night they all came, and after having been amused with dances and a bonfire, they were complimented with an entertainment, which lasted beyond midnight. Since that day, the English visited the Navvab several times, and at each time several complaints, and many reproaches were taking place on both sides; and at each visit matters seemed verging towards a rupture. For it was remarked, that at every meeting, the Navvab, whether by chance or otherwise, never failed to commit some action, or to be guilty of some gesture, which never failed to give offence, and to be laid hold of as a fit subject of complaint. At last, the discontents ran so high, that at one time Mr. Amyatt, who had advanced as far as the door of the Navvab's apartment, returned back much displeased; nor would he have been brought again, had not some of the Navvab's favourites run after him, and intreated his being pacified. Mr. Amyatt and the others complained of the Navvab's guards at the gate, and of some other of his servants. The Navvab professed his ignorance, and made many apologies; but the English could not be brought to believe, that servants would dare to commit such actions without their master's consent; and they were still more displeased at the apology. However, as the Navvab was offering many excuses, they determined that the only method with him was, to put his words to the trial. With that view, Mr. Gulston and Captain Johnston, got on horse-back at daybreak, as is the English custom, and went out to take an airing, and to see the country; but as soon as they offered to go somewhat far, several foot-guards, stationed at that part, forbade their proceeding that way; and some troopers, that suddenly appeared, opposed their passage. The English, accustomed to talk high, and to carry every thing with a high hand, forced their passage forward. The guards incensed, lighted up their matches and put themselves in a posture of defence; and the English, after having attempted in vain to turn them, returned to town, and went directly to the Navvab's where they exhaled themselves in excessive complaints, and made use of several high expressions. The Navvab flatly denied his having any hand in the matter, and excused his people; he also apologised for himself, and pretended his ignorance. But this did not persuade any one of the English; nor was this dust wiped off from their hearts; and this

36. He was Mr. Amyatt's speaker and linguist; but, having at the very first interview expressed himself with roughness, and been all the while looking at the Navvab which with that imperiousness was then the general style, that Prince refused to speak to him any more. Amyatt's temper, air, looks, and tone of voice, as well as his style of speech, may be conjectured from that single ancedote. It is observable, that the few English, who in those days understood the Persian and Hindostany, and Vansittart was master of the former spoke it so strangely, and in such a tone of voice, that Mir-cassem, unable to understand Vansittart, was obliged to make use of a liguist.—[Translator's Note.]

event having alienated their minds, their discontent ran higher and higher, and at last it undermined the wall of good will and sincerity. The Navvab was every day holding Councils on these matters with his favourites; for instance, with Aaly-hibrahim-qhan, and with Mirza-shems-eddin. Those men of sense always proposed some expedient to renew the conferences, in order both to soothe Mr. Amyatt's mind, and to pacify the Navvab. On my own part, as I laboured under the imputation of being in connection with the English, I did not dare to offer a word in their behalf; but being also intimate with Aaly-hibrahim-qhan, and with Mirza-shems-eddin, I used to impart to them such expedients and notions of mine, as I thought might conduce to a good understanding, or keep at a distance the thoughts of hostility, and these were soon imparted to the Navvab, who always assented, but not for any length of time. For as soon as it was four in the afternoon, at which time Gurghin-qhan used to come and to engross him as late as nine o'clock at night, all was undone again; so that he would efface himself every trace of those lines, which his well-wishers had been at so much pains to trace on the glass of his mind; and in the morning, not the least vestige of them could be discerned. Instead of that, the General used to engrave thereon his own infructuous persuasions, and that too, in such deep characters, that no hand and no tool could efface them afterwards. This management took place so constantly, that once Aaly-hibrahim-qhan losing all patience, wrote a note to the Navvab in these very words: *Since the advices and counsels offered by your well-wishers, and which your mind approves, never fail in the evening to be obliterated by Gurghin-ghan's suggestions, it is needless that either your Highness, or your friends and well-wishers, should fatigue themselves any more upon an unfructuous subject; for in the end, we all find that nothing is done, but what has been advised by Guaghin-qhan. It is then proper that this affair should be wholly committed to his care, without giving further trouble to your own mind, as well as to every one of us on so disagreeable a subject. Let us all do as he shall bid;* (and this after all would be nothing novel) *it is but what happens every day. In one word,* (for we must end) *we are unanimously of opinion, that if your Princely mind be for peace, Mr. Amyatt's heart ought not to be estranged by actions and words that derogate from the high charactor which our master bears; and, if you be for a rupture, and for pursue a plan of military operations on Gurghin-ghan's notions and schemes, still, to disoblige a man come on an embassy, is contrary to the rules of a Princely behaviour, and beneath the high dignity of a Sovereign. So far from abating any thing from the regard and attention which it is customary to pay the people of that nation, we are of opinion that some additional token of respect ought to be shewn them now, were it because they are come under the safeguard of an embassy. We do not mean to say that the preparations intended for further hostilities ought to be discontinued; on the contrary, they ought to go on. We contend only, that such actions as these men complain of, are not of a nature either to add any thing to the terror of your name and power, or to detract any thing from their own dignity, or from the opinion they entertain of themselves. All these can produce no other fruit than that of enlarging the foundations of enmity, and giving new wings to envy and jealousy.*

"Gurghin-qhan having somehow got advice of this note of Aaly-hibrahim-qhan's took offence at it, and for two or three days together he abstained from coming to Court. It was just at this time that a boat from Calcutta came to touch at Monghyr. She proved to be laden with a quantity of goods, under which were found five hundred fire-locks, destined for the factory of Azim-abad. These Gurghin-qhan wanted to stop, whilst Mr. Amyatt insisted upon the boat's being dismissed without being stopped or even searched; and to that forbearance the Court would not listen. Aaly-hibarhim-qhan objected to the boat's being stopped or visited at all. He contended, "That if peace was in "contemplation, there was no colour for stopping the boat; and if hostilities were in view, then he "saw no great harm in adding five hundred more musquets to the two thousand already in the "English factory. For if we can fight against two thousand," said he, "I dare say, we can as well "fight against two thousand five hundred." To this the Navvab having said that he wondered why nobody would say so much to Gurghin-qhan himself, Aaly-hibrahim-qhan answered, that if His Highness's pleasure was that so much should be said to Gurghin-qhan, it would prove a small affair. The Navvab, a little affected by these words, desired Radja Nobet-rày and Aaly-hibrahim-qhan to go and bring Gurghin-qhan to Court, as he intended to consult him on this subject. The two Lords accepted the commission, and departed. Gurghin-qhan, on hearing their errand, seemed to be in a passion, and said, "My office is that of Grand-master of the artillery, and I am but a soldier; nor "have I any business with consultations and politics. Let His Highness consult with his friends "and favourites. Whenever there is war, and I am sent to stand in some post, I hope, I shall not "fail to do my duty; but as for politics, I know nothing of them." The Radja observing the violence of the man's temper, said not a word, but turned his eyes towards Aaly-hibrahim-qhan. The Qhan having chided Gurghin-qhan a little upon his ill humour, said these very words: "The Navvab-aaly-"djáh asks advice from his Grand-master of the artillery, and it appears that he never transacts "business without consulting him. Why then does not the Grand-master of the artillery give such "advice as he thinks best for his own honour, and for his master's service?" These words having somewhat pacified Gurghin-qhan, he turned himself towards Aaly-hibrahim-qhan, and raised both his hands, which he set open against each other. He explained his thought by this comparison or allegory: "*The Navvab and the English,*" said he, "*stand now in this manner: that is, they are "upon a par and an equality, and on the same level; but if he does not stand firm, and chooses to "lower his tone a little,* (and here he sunk his right a little) *the other hand will remain where it is; "and of course higher. If, on the contrary, his hand remains where it is, the English hand must fall "lower, and the Navvab will remain with a superiority on his side. As to the rest, let His Highness "do as he pleases; he is the master.*" The envoys returned to the Navvab with this answer, and they reported the whole transaction minutely; but this opinion of the General's having put an end to all thoughts about pacification, nothing was thought of now but a rupture, and open hostilities. So that Mr. Amyatt finding it useless to make any further stay, resolved to return, and he took his leave. The Navvab at first wanted to keep every one of the English, as hostages; at last, after a deal of parley, he consented to dismiss them all, under condition that Mr. Hay should be detained at Monghyr, until Mirza-mahmed-aaly and some other of the Navvab's officers confined at Calcutta, should be released, and upon their way to Monghyr; at which time he would release Mr. Hay. The latter having consented (and this consent of his became in the sequel the cause of his death), Mr. Amyatt and the others obtained leave, and went down the river in their boats."

---

14. THE MURDER OF AMYATT.

The circumstances of Amyatt's murder are still involved in obscurity. The diaries gives us one account; the *Seir-i-Mutaqherin* gives us another. Perhaps M. Raymond, the translator of the *Seir-i Mutaqherin* may be trusted.

"What to think of this narrative of our author's but, that he was then far from the scene of action, or possibly wrote this narrative some years later? The Navvab's order being to send Amyatt with his retinue to Monghyr, Mahmedtaky-qhan betook himself to the following expedient, to execute the commission with ease, and without tumult: Being then encamped on the Bagraty, between Murshid-abad and Cassimbazar, as soon as the boats were descried, he sent his friend and steward, Aga-aaly-toork, to invite Amyatt to an entertainment. Amyatt excused himself, and continued pushing in the middle of the stream. Another message was sent by a person of still greater consequence, who represented, that the entertainment being ready, the General would think himself aggrieved by the disappointment. Amyatt, having again excused himself, the envoy returned; and, on his landing, the boat-men were hailed from shore, and *ordered* to bring to. This order was answered by two musket-balls, and then by a volley, which being answered from shore the boats were immediately boarded, and such a scene of slaughter ensued, as is hardly so be described ; as Amyatt, by his eternal instigations, as well as by his very haughty temper, was reputed the author of the rupture. All these particulars I know from the report then general ; from Aga-aaly, who has been my friend and neighbour, for full sixteen years ; from the Secretary and servants of the General's ; and lastly, from three women, from amongst the five sets of dance-girls, that had been assembled on the occasion."

The murder of Amyatt[37] seems to have taken place on either the 3rd or 4th of July, 1763.

---

15. THE EVENTS RECORDED IN THE DIARIES.

This Introduction has now gone as far as can be required of an Introduction. It has brought the reader up to the date at which the Diaries commence. It would have been tempting to have gone further, to have summarised the Diaries, and to have shown how the outrage against humanity they record was faithfully and fully avenged, but to attempt this would require a greater expenditure of money in printing than the Society can at this present time meet. Neither can I devote any pages to the biography of the men who play no important a part in this tragedy. The reader must think of Ellis as far more of a soldier than a civil servant. At the seige of Calcutta in 1756 he had held an Ensign's commission, and distingiushed himself by his bravery. He distinguished himself in Clive's too little known fight at Sealdah, on which occasion he was reported dead, but survived with the loss of a leg.[38] Peter Carstairs also, had covered himself with glory at the siege of Calcutta and had fought at Plassey. Henry Lushington endured the Black Hole, was Clive's accomplice in the trick played upon Amichand—he was but eighteen years old when he picked the half-dead body of Holwell from among the dead in the Black Hole Prison. Of Gulston, the Persian translator, it is related, that when after the first massacre, the remains of the victims were being cast down a well in the courtyard, his body being discovered, he was found to be still alive. The men were inclined to have saved him ; but, writes Broome, "this gentleman, who was an admirable linguist, smarting with his wounds and ignorant of their kindly intentions towards him, gave them abuse and threatened them with the vengeance of his countymen, upon which they threw him still breathing into the well with his more fortunate companians."

Of Sumroo so much has been written, that I must be content to refer the reader to Mr. H. Compton's *European Military Adventures of Hindustan.* (Appendix 4.)

As to Fullarton, in addition to what has been said above, I will only venture to quote the following passage from Lt.-Col. D. G. Crawford's interesting paper *Lists of Surgeons in India in 1749.*

" *William Fullerton* plays a more prominent part in history than any of his medical contemporaries, except Holwell. He was appointed one of the Surgeons to the Calcutta General Hospital, succeeding Holwell, in 1744. "The President proposed and ordered the appointment of Mr. John

---

37. Peter Amyatt (spelt Amyat, Amyati Amiot etc.) Arrived 2nd August 1742, when he must have been about 15 years old. At the time of the downfall of Calcutta, he was Chief of the Council at Jagdea ; he escaped on board a sloop to Fulta, having rescued about Rs 60,000 worth of the Company's effects. He formed one of the Council of Fulta, and Holwell on his arrival at that place expressed the opinion that Amyatt had been "the only person invested with any just title to conduct the affairs and concerns of the Company......until the arrival of the gentlemen of the Board of Calcutta, who lay under no censure or suspicion from the service" This Holwell thought was the consequence of Drake, etc , having abondoned the Fort in the hour of danger. Early in February, 1757. Amyatt was sent by Clive with letters to the Nawab, then in the neighbourhood of Dum Dum. He was one of the agents for the Military on the capture of Calcutta. In 1760 Amyatt went to Patna as Chief. The Amyatts were evidently a well established family in Calcutta, and their house is shown in one of the maps of Calcutta given in Wilson's *Old Fort William.* On April 6th 1763 he had married a Miss Maria Woolaston, who, after Peter's death, married her late husband's executor—Captain James Amyatt.

38. Broome *Op. Cit.* p. 391 writes of the first Patna massacre : "Neither age nor sex was spared, and Sumroo consummated his diabolical villany by the murder of Mr. Ellis' infant child, from which it may be inferred as probable that Mrs. Ellis was amongst the victims."

Knox, but the majority did not approve of the appointment." (Letter from Bengal, dated 23rd August 1750, paras. 30 and 61.) He was in Calcutta at the time of its siege and capture, in 1756, but appears to have been on board one of the ships, on professional duty, at the time of the Governor's flight. On 8th December 1757 he was appointed Mayor of Calcutta for the ensuing year. In a letter, dated 1st September 1760, he resigned his Surgeoncy at Calcutta; after which he was appointed Surgeon to the Patna Agency. He greatly distinguished himself during the war in Behar, both in the action at Masimpur, on 9th February 1760, and in the subsequent siege of Patna. (Broome, *History of the Bengal Army*, Vol. I, pp. 281-293, and p. 297, these services are also mentioned in the *Seir-i-Mutaqherin*, translation, Vol. III, pp. 340 and 350). Fullerton was taken prisoner, with the other English Officers there, when Patna was captured by Nawab Kasim Ali in 1763; and was the only man spared, when all the rest perished in the Patna massacre. (Broome, p. 392, also *Seir-i-Mutaqherin*. Vol. II, p. 506.) Subsequently he fell into bad odour with the Government. Two letters from Bengal, dated 16th January 1761, paragraphs 6—8, and 30th October 1762, paragraphs 85—93, speak of him unfavourably. 'Mr. Fullerton, formerly Surgeon, has been of late Nandcoomar's associate. He has always been at the head of a party, and has now taken his passage home in the *Latham*. He is suspected of encouraging the correspondence to promote the disaffection of the Burdwan Rajah. Mr. Fullerton is a great bane to Society, and the Company's Service; so much is said of him that he may not on any account be suffered to return.' In spite of having taken his passage in the *Latham*, he remained in India at least up to March 1766. The actual charge against him appears to have been as follows :—Nandkumar wrote to Raja Bulwant Singh, advising him against an alliance with the English. General Carnac wished Nandkumar to be removed from the Nawab's service. Fullerton acted as interpreter at on enquiry held into Nandkumar's conduct, knew of this letter, and did not mention it. He appears to have been censured only, for a letter from him is extant in the Calcutta Record Office, dated 21st March 1766, in which he answers the censure passed on him in the Consultations of 24th February 1766. This is the last definitely dated mention of Fullerton which I know of. He appears to have been on terms of intimate personal friendship with Syed Gulam Husain Khan, the author of the *Seir-i-Mutaqherin*, who constantly refers to their friendship in the second volume. In Vol. III. p. 7 he mentions Fullerton for the last time."

In an article on "Surgeons in India—Past and Present" which appeared in the *Calcutta Review* for July, 1854, I find an extract from a letter written by Dr. Anderson "of the Infantry" to his friend Dr. Davidson and with this passage this Introduction may well close.

"Since my last his Excellency has been completely defeated, and in consequence obliged to retreat to Jaffier Khan's (Jafar Khan's) gardens, yesterday, and proposes coming into the city, this day (9th October, 1763)[39] Sumroo, with his sepoys arrived here last night, and I suppose to effect his wicked designs; for Mr. Kelly[40] and forty-three gentlemen with him were massacred, and an equal number of soldiers, and us yet remain: I expect my fate this night. Dear D., this is no surprise to me, for I expected it all along. I must, therefore, as a dying man, request of you to collect and remit my estate home as soon as possible, and write a comforting letter to my father and mother; let them know I die bravely as a Christian ought, and for I fear not him that kill the body and no more, but I rejoice in hope of a future existence through the merits of my Saviour."

39. It will be seen that the first massacre took place on October 5th.

40. Ellis?

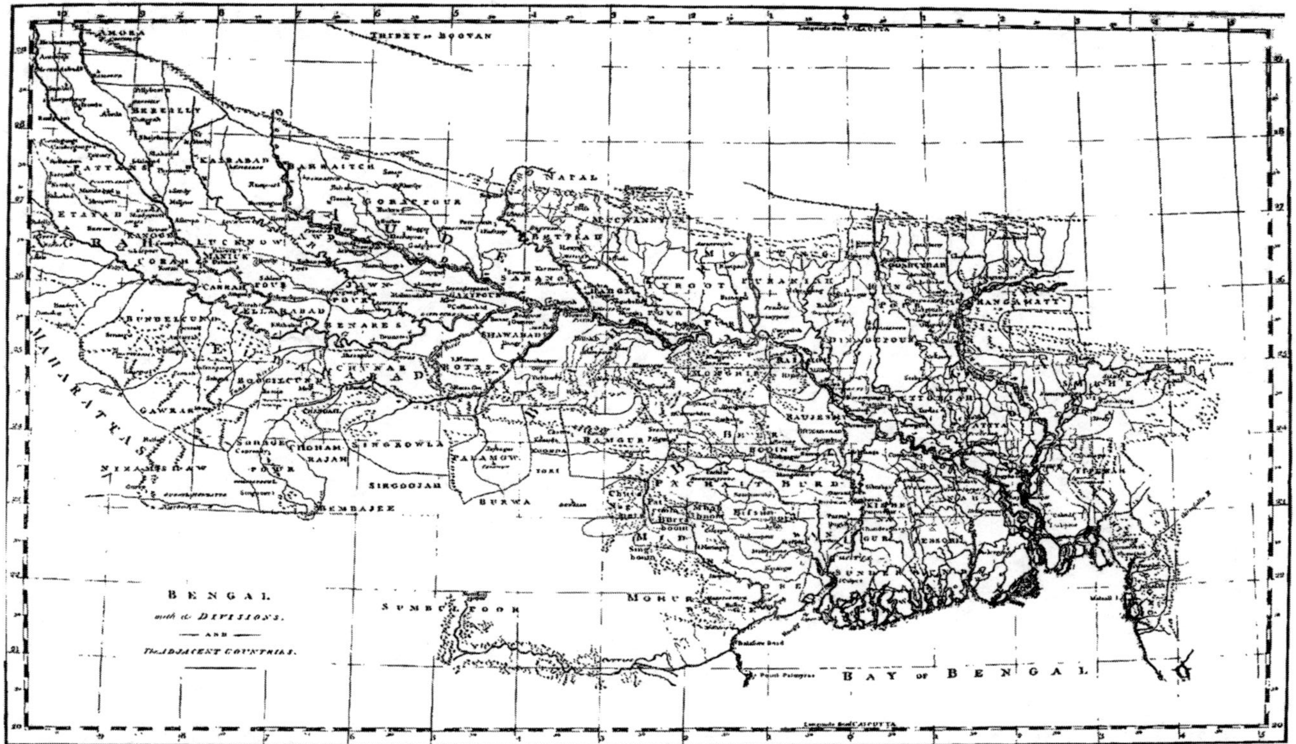

From Orme's "History of the Military Transactions in Indostan."
(Fourth Edition, [illegible]).

The Diaries of Three Surgeons of Patna,

1763.

The Diaries of Three Surgeons of Patna 1763.

THE DIARY OF SURGEON ANDERSON.

June 23rd.—Being the anniversary of the Battle of Plassey, we all dined at the Factory when it was easy to observe by the faces of the gentlemen that somewhat of importance was on the carpet: for our council had been sitting, and orders were issued out for the guards to be relieved by the awkwardmen, and the captains to meet the Commanding Officer at his quarters at 8 in the evening. It seems the gentlemen of the factory had the advice of Mr. Amyatt's negotiations at Mongheer being broken off and a day appointed for his departure, also that a strong detachment of horse and sepoys, to the number of 3,000, with six guns were on the March to Patna, so that a war seemed inevitable, they thought it best to strike the first sroke by possessing themselves of the city of Patna. However, they were willing to wait for certain advices from Mr Amyatt; accordingly, the 24th at night.

June 24th—in consequence of that advice, orders were given to attack the city next morning.

THE DIARY OF SURGEON PETER CAMPBELL.

June 23rd 1763.—This day I dined at the Factory with most of the officers, etc., in commemoration of the battle of Placey (*sic*) when I observed by the private conferences of Messrs. Ellis, Carstairs, etc., that the public embroils, which have been long threatening appeared to be coming near to a crisis, which made me take Carstairs, aside and ask him whether he thought I was safe to stay longer in the city; he told me, for that night I may, but no longer, and invited me out to his garden.

June 24th. -This morning I employed myself in settling matters with my *banyan* and getting my things sent out to Captain Carstairs'; dined at the Factory, where the gentlemen kept everything very private; arrived at Carstairs about 4 o'clock; upon inquiry of him I understood that they intended attacking the city to-morrow morning, but he had just received a chit from Mr. Ellis, wherein he mentioned he had received intelligence by the *cossid* that Mr. Amyatt had been entertained by the Nabob with a *notch* and came home highly pleased; wherefore he thought their intentions of attack should be deferred till he heard from Mr. Amyatt himself, which he expected that evening, and should then give him

SURGEON FULLARTON'S NARRATIVE OF THE PROCEEDINGS AT PATNA.

(*Received and read in Council the 19th December, 1763.*)

From the 17th of the month of June preparations of war were carried on with great vigour on both sides. Mindialy Ali Cawn, who governed this city, was employed in repairing the ramparts, clearing the ditch, and posting troops on the walls, and doubling all the guards to the westward of the city. The Factory walls were likewise repaired, the ditch was cleared, and the 24-pounders were mounted; the terrace top of the Factory house, which was all round, fortified with sand bags, and two 3-pounders were mounted there.

June 24th.—About 10 o'clock at night on the 24th June, Mr. Ellis sent for me from the hospital, and ordered that the sick might be embarked in boats and carried over to the sand opposite to the city, and from thence tracked up, and crossed over to the Factory. My orders were to embark at 2 o'clock in the morning (that being the hour appointed for the attack of the city).

June 25th.—About one, the troops were under arms and marched off : at two (about two companies of awkward men with two Officers left at the gardens for a guard) in the following order :—Captain Tabby's seapoys and the Europeans were to march to the right / by the road* of the chota Montenal / Mutni* bastion with their scaling ladders and enter there. Captains Turner and Wilson with four companies each and two pieces of cannon were to proceed to the west gate, enter there, while Lieutenant Downie with three companies escaladed opposite the factory. Captain Kinch, with remainder of the guns, was stationed in Mr. Howitt's compound in order to fire upon he walls, and be as a signal for a general attack. Three pieces (three pounders) with two companies of seapoys were to keep up a constant fire from the top of the factory house. Captain Carstairs with the Europeans and Tabby's seapoys after entering, passed along the north-west front and opened the gates, so that the other party with the two guns passed in without any difficulty. We possessed ourselves soon of all the bastions, but had great difficulty in going up the great street as there was a great fire from the houses in which we lost some men and officers, but at length proceeded to the *killa* into which the only force in the city had retired. The Subah with most of his zemindars had left the city, and we now began to think ourselves secure, but alas ! how greatly mistaken. Lieutenants Downie and Perry, with some seapoys had gone quite through the *killa* to the outer side. Our Europeans were in possession of the east gate with one of our guns, but all the rest of our

immediate notice. Betwixt 8 and 9 a message arrived that he had leave of the Nabob to proceed to Calcutta on the 24th ; wherefore he ordered the attack should be made on the morning as they formerly agreed. Most of the officers supped with Carstairs and I came into the Factory betwixt eleven and twelve and found all the gentlemen making all preparation for the attack.

June 25th.—The army moved from Bankipore at 2 o'clock in the morning, and they judged in the factory that the army would reach the city before 4. Accordingly, about a quarter to 4, we heard a firing, upon which a party of sepoys, which was stationed on the top of the factory house, was ordered to keep up a constant fire upon the rampart of the wall next the factory, and two 3-pounders, which was (*sic*), also there, were ordered to play away upon the same rampart, and the two 24 pounders below kept up an incessant fire till daylight (all this period a very little firing was returned from the city, as I believe they were all asleep when attacked). We now observed all the walls lined with our colours and sepoys, which to be sure, in our situation, was very agreeable, and every minute furnished us with the agreeable news of everything going before us ; in short by 9 we were confidently assured that we were in possession of every post ; then our great folks began to look into the administration of the province ; perwannahs were issuing to the Phousdars to continue their former obedience in sending in provisions, etc., to the city as formerly. Naissars were coming in plenty to the Chief, and joy reigned in the face of everybody. Biscuits, wine, etc., were sent in to the officers to refresh them ; numbers of wounded men were now coming out of the city, which employed Messrs. Fullarton, Anderson, and self for the day ; surmises now passed that we had not as yet got possession of the Killa, and by 12 was confirmed. About 2 o'clock Carstairs and Kinch came to the Factory, and acquainted us that we were beat out of the city, and that it was not in their power to make one man stand ; which was the case, for by

June 25th.—which was accordingly executed, and with the sick, which consisted of 23 Europeans, got safe to the Factory about 9 o'clock in the morning. At half an hour before one, the troops under the command of Captain Carstairs marched from the Cantonments in two divisions ; and Captain Carstairs having sent 50 sepoys, 25 to each of the grand roads at 11 the night of the 24th June, to take everybody that might pass that way till the arrival of the troops. They took 50 prisoners, great many of whom were *harcarrahs*, by which means they had not the least intelligence in the city ; the first commanded by Captain Carstairs, consisting of 150 Europeans, Captain Tabby's battalion of sepoys, and five Companies of Captain Wilson's, the second division consisted of 50 Europeans, Captain Turner's battalion of sepoys and two guns. The first division, with the scaling ladders, came down the great Western Road ; the second came through the town right down to the West Gate and there remained under cover. The first division planted their ladders near the south-west bastion of the city ; they mounted and got in with little opposition and little loss ; they marched down along the walls to the west gate, which they opened (our guns and small arms keeping a constant fire from the factory upon the city), and the second division and the guns came in. Lieutenant Downie. who commanded in the factory with three companies of sepoys, a little after our troops had got the possession of the west gate, stormed the Barbuna gate, got in with little loss, and marched through the killa, partly by the riverside, partly by the lanes near the river. Captain Tabby with his battalion went round het

* Note the passage above is the Calcutta text that below Mr. Beveridge's text.

sepoys were dispersed and plundering, so that scarce one hundred could be got together.

Every body was / all were* quite fatigued, having marched through thick mud, and had no refreshment, when near 1 o'clock, about 120 of the enemy entered the *killa* and drove some seapoys who were there before them. The Europeans and other seapoys seeing this, followed their example and so scarce looked back till they got to the factory; a party of Marcott's seapoys who belonged to the detachment sent to re-inforce the city, arrived with some guns soon after, and began to fire on the factory house. Thus ended this unhappy affair, and not without great loss and effusion of blood. The enemy must have suffered much, but can give no particulars. Our loss is as follows:—

Killed—Captain Perry, Lieutenants Downie, McDonnal, Reed / McDowel, Roach, and about eight Europeans.

Wounded—Captains Jocher / Joecher, Willson, Lieutenant Perry, 10 Europeans and 100 sepoys.

Killed and deserted, but mostly the latter, and I believe loaded with plunder one thousand sepoys with officers in proportion. Lost two field pieces which could not be brought off. Our whole force consisted of 150 Europeans, rank-and-file, 40 artillery, 2,200 seapoys.

At six in the evening, the guard for the gardens was called in, and arrived soon after. After this disaster a / the council was called, in which the Captains were desired to attend that they might consult of what was best to be done in our present circumstances. Various were the opinions on this occasion. First the factory being but small and badly provided with provisions and firewood for 1,200 seapoys and 200 Europeans, besides we must have expected to have been entirely shut up with the fresh troops which would have come from Mongheer, therefore to defend it was thought to no purpose. Second, to take boats and proceed by water to Calcutta, but in all accounts less than a hundred men drove our whole army out, and this sad misfortune was entirely owing to the plundering of our seapoys and soldiers, which turned their courage into avarice, and everyone of them thought of nothing but sculking off with what they got. By 3 most of the scattered army returned into the Factory. Our army consisted as follows:—

Europeans, half rank and file ...	47	
Artillery, ditto ...	19	
	66	... 198

Besides officers.

Seapoys	... 2,500
Total	... 2,698

Returned from the attack.

Europeans, half rank and file ...	42	
Artillery ditto ...	14	
	56	.. 168
Seapoys		... 1,200
Total		... 1,368

Europeans killed, wounded, and missing	35
Artillery, killed wounded, and missing	6
Seapoys wounded	100
Do. killed	150
Total ...	291

Officers Killed.

Captain Parry.	Lieutenant McDonall.
Lieutenant Downey.	Artillery, Lieut. Ried.

walls and drove the enemy from them, posting his own guards as he went and came to the east gate. By the time both our division had got into the city, Mirza Mindialy Cawn, the Governor, had intelligence of it and collected a body of horse and gunmen, and marching down the main street, he met Captain Carstairs with Captain Turner's sepoys, Europeans and guns. He lined the streets, and filed the lanes, and the tops of the houses of both sides. Captain Parry and Lieutenant McDowall were both killed, Captains Jocher and Wilson were wounded, 30 Europeans killed and wonded with a number of sepoys. But our grape and musketry were so warm that they retired and Mindialy Cawn, with the rest of the Cammanders, went out by the east gate of the city, and took the road towards Fatwa. Our troops marched to the east gate after them and there met Captain Tabby, who had just arrived having come round the walls. The east gate was immediately shut, the bridge leading into it broke down, and the sepoys went along the killa walls to the river side, and took possession of the only gate remaining in the hands of the enemy, called the water gate. After this, several messages passed between Captain Carstairs and Mr. Ellis, and everything seemed to be over. About 9 o'clock Carstairs came to the factory with several of the officers. At ten we heard firing in the killa, and the gentlemen went to the fort, the firing continued and increased. One Lal Singh, a jamadar of foot, who had his women in a house in the killa, did not choose to leave them, so retired into his house with thirty men, and remained quiet till some of our sepoys began to plunder his houses; he then in defence of his women drove them out; there were likewise about 200 men who secreted themselves in a large house near the killa, called Chahalsatun. Lal Singh after having driven the sepoys from his house, fired on the sentries that were posted on the walls of the killa near his house, and sent a message to Mindialy Cawn, who with the rest of the principal commanders had got the length of the Fatwa bridge, to drive the English out

* Note the passage above is the Calcutta text that below Mr. Beveridge's text.

the first place boats could not be procured for such a number, and must have expected an opposition at Mongheer, where intelligence must arrive one day before us. Third, to cross the river and march down on the opposite side. This must have been to sacrifice many, as we must have embarked in the face of a numerous enemy who had doubtless troops opposite Mongheer to meet us, besides it was impossible without bullocks or coolies to have either guns or much ammunition with us. Therefore the final determination, and indeed that which had the most chance of succeeding, was to procure by force as many boats as we could, send them up to Phytazi / Phylagi Pass, and cross the river with one howitz, march up the Sarear Sarang / Sircar Saran country, and so cross over to Sujah Dowlat's country. This was approved of, but the boats could not be procured that night, and the day following :—

Officers Wounded.

Captain Wilson. | Captain Yeagar.
Lieutenant Parry.

The great deficiency in the Seapoys is owing to their desertion with their plunder. After this melancholy accident everybody was greatly nonplussed what was the most prudent step to be taken ; (as in such case) numbers of schemes were proposed, and none could determine what was the most advisable ; at last it was fixed to proceed to Sujad-Dawla's province, but a great difficulty arose in the procuring of boats. At last with much trouble there were collected as many as we thought would do, and agreed to sett off the next morning.

of the city. Mindialy Cawn met at Fatwa with Alum Cawn, 100 horse, 20 camels loaded with fine arrows sent from Mongheer for his garrison, just at the time of his receiving Lal Singh's message. We immediately returned, and by the way picked about 1,000 horse and foot that were flying from the city. At the same time that Lal Singh sent to Mindialy Cawn, he sent likewise to the Chahalsatun, and told those men men that were there that he had still defended that part of the *killa* and desired their assistance. About fifty of them came to him by a small passage from the Chahalsetoon to the *killa*, and there they defended themselves till near 12 o'clock, when Mindialy Cawn arrived. About this time our soldiers were employed in plundering the town and little order or obedience to their officers was observed, nor could a sufficient body of them be got together to make a stand, so that Mindialy Cawn met with little resistance in driving all our troops out of the city. As our people went along, they met with enemies everywhere : the sepoys who had concealed themselves in the different houses, upon hearing of the Nabob's return, sallied out everywhere and fired on them, so that, at about 3 o'clock they arrived at the Factory in the utmost confusion, having lost in the retreat Lieutenant Reed of the Artillery, Lieutenant Downie of the sepoys and Lieutenant Parry wounded. Several attempts were made by the officers to rally both the sepoys and the Europeans, but to no purpose ; it was generally imagined that great part of the sepoys were gone off with the plunder they had got, and that night, at a muster, there were only about 170 Europeans and 1,200 sepoys to be found. The confusion of such a number of troops with the sick and wounded in so small a place at the Factory must be easily imagined ; and that evening about sunset the city was strongly enforced by Marcod with 1,500 sepoys and two guns and some horse, who that night began to ply us with musketry from the walls and cannonading of the Factory from the west gate. Messrs. Greentree and Pickering were called in from the Cantonments, where they had been left with 200 new seapoys.

June 26th.—Having got as many boats as we could and sent them up to the Pass, we prepared everything for evacuating the Factory. In the interim a very brisk and incessant fire of both great guns and musketry was kept on both sides in which we lost a European and three or four seapoys. About ten at night we got our sick Europeans and treasure—about one lakh—embarked. Soon after Captain Tabby's seapoys were ordered to march out to the sand to the north of the French factory and there wait for the Europeans. Mr. Ellis, with a company of seapoys from that body, attended by some civilians, made the best of their way to the boats. Captain Carstairs, with the Europeans, and Turner's seapoys kept up a brisk fire till near 12 o'clock, and everything being quite ready, spiked the guns, etc., and marched out and so proceeded to the boats without the least molestation.

June 26th.—This morning a very brisk cannonade was kept up by both us and the city, they having mounted some 6-pounders of ours which fell into their hands. We had two or three killed. The whole day a constant fire was continued, everything was got in readiness for our departure by evening that could be done in our confused situation; they found it unpracticable to carry any guns, the reason I don't know; but we carried an howitet, but no shells, the reason of that I don't know; both of which we experimented afterwards, would have been of the utmost consequence to us. Our treasure amounted to pretty near a lakh; that was shipped off, but by some mis-management our boat, that part of it was put in, sunk as she was setting off, and with difficulty saved; the other was too deep and run aground, which obliged them to throw some of it overboard, so that there was deficient 20,000 Rupees the first night. We carried only 25 barrels ammunition, which we found not to behalf sufficient for the work we met with afterwards. About 9 o'clock Captain Tabby was sent out with his battalion to draw up on the sand opposite the French factory, to cover our retreat. Afterwards Mr. Ellis, with some of the civilians and your humble servant, came off and got a company of Tabby's seapoys, and marched tofi nd the boats, which was about four or five *coss*, and to our great mortification did not find them at the place we imagined them to have been. The Europeans left the Factory about eleven, and then our whole shattered army proceeded, and fortunately fell in with us while we was in our dilemma about the boats.

June 26th.—In the morn.ng, the fire from the city increased, and the confusion with us was greater. Early in the morning, Mr. Ellis sent for me, and ordered me to go over to the sand opposite to the Factory with 50 sepoys and collect all the boats I could get. The fire was very warm both from the Factory and the city all that day. About 12 o'clock I was ordered to proceed with what boats I had collected to Phaleza Ghat, about 3 *coss* up the river, and there to remain for further orders. At three in the afternoon I was ordered to get the boats ready for transporting the troops over to the Sarkar Sarun country as soon as possible. At ten at night they arrived, in number about 700 Europeans and 1,000 sepoys with a howitzer. Our troops, on leaving the Factory, set fire to the gunge and all the large betelnut bungalows near the Factory to hinder the enemy's approach, and an officer with 30 Europeans remained in the Factory half an hour after the main body marched off to bring up the rear with the baggage. But the fire from the city was so warm that the coolies and lascars threw most part of the ammunition down and deserted, so that only seven barrels of musket ammunition were saved, and the sepoys and Europeans had only 12 rounds a man.

June 27th.—About two, we began to cross as quick as possible and without confusion, but before one-third were over it began to blow and rain, so that the boats could not cross. In the meantime, those that had crossed were alarmed by a body of horse coming to attack them. They beat to arms got the howitz ready, and advanced 200 or 300 yards to be clear off the village, and so waited for them, but they thought proper to keep at a distance. About ten, the weather turned fair and wind moderate, so that on the afternoon every-

June 27th.—We all proceeded up the river, and at about three found the boats, and immediately began to embark, and was not complet till ten. We halted at a village on the opposite side, and rested till five, and marched six *coss*, and halted on the road for the remainder of the night. Most of the boats proceeded up the river with the wounded Europeans, Lady Hope, Howett, Doctors Fullarton and Anderson, *cum multis aliis*.

June 27th.—About daylight in the morning, the troops got all to the other side of the river to halt there for Mr. Lushington, who had embarked from the Factory with the Company's treasure in small packages. He arrived at 10 o'clock with only the loss of one boat, which was sank by the enemy's shot at the Factory ghât. A little before sunset we marched from Phaleza to Raipati, being four *coss*, where the army got no provisions, but a little rice, the country people being afraid to supply us on account

body was crossed over, even our horses. We began to prepare for marching. Accordingly, the sick, treasure, and howitz with part of the ammunition were to go by water for want of coolies, etc., while the army marched by land; on account of the sick I went by water. In the afternoon, about 5 o'clock, the army marched, and we got under sail with a fair wind, being about thirty boats in all. Here I was greatly disappointed for the boat with my clothes, instruments, medicines, and servants did not arrive, so that I imagine this must have been stopped. We sailed the best part of the night and then came to.

June 28th.—At daylight got under way and halted at Chasan/Cherand Soon after we were all alarmed with two or three companies of seapoys, which we discovered on the opposite shore, and observing them drawing some boats together, we sent immediate advice to Mr. Ellis, who sent a company of seapoys to reinforce us, for we had only fifty. About five, the army joined us.

June 29th.—Early got under way, but our *budgero* being heavy, we generally brought up the rear. Those seapoys of the enemy having got three boats, chased us about 8 o'clock, but having a fresh wind, and by help of our oars we happily got clear. A guard boat and another in our rear fell in with them. The former cleared herself after a brisk fire, but the other was taken, the seapoys having jumped over board, after having two men killed and two wounded. We entered this afternoon the river *Dowie* (a name of the Gogra), brought to within a *coss* of the army about three *coss* above Chupra.

June 28th.—At daybreak we marched about one *coss*, and reached a village, where we halted and refreshed till 3. We found in the Phousdar's house a tent and a cammel, which we used the liberty to carry along with us and some carriage bullocks. We marched about five *coss* and found our boats at this village and halted for the night.

June 29th.—At half past two this morning we marched and our boats proceeded up. We reached Chuppera about 8. A few of us stopped at our Factory house and found about three dozen of different liquors, which was a most agreeable acquisition, as we had not brought a drop along with us; found also some turkeys and other poultry. We proceeded on about a *coss* further, and halted in a *tope*, and sent out and got some bullocks and rice for our people. We were alarmed and under arms, two or three, different times that a party of horse was near us. We understood that the Phousdar, one Ramneedie, had collected about 1,000 troops and 200 horse. We marched at 4, and halted at a *tope* about four *coss* from hence. Captain Turner, who had the rear guard, informed us that just as he left the ground, a party of the enemy's horse took possession of it, which made us keep a good look out all night We had intelligence from our boats that they were pursued by some of our enemy from the Bhoodgepur side, and that they had taken two of these small boats; indeed, two seapoys that

of the Phousdar's (Ram Nidi) being in arms to oppose us. Mr. Ellis ordered me to take charge of the treasure with all the boats, and allotted for their guard one company of sepoys; the boat had a fine wind and sailed all night.

June 28th.—The boats were fired on from the Bhojpur side of the country by Shimroo, who was then preparing to cross the river to attack us. No news of the troops till 3 o'clock in the afternoon, when they arrived at Chirand where the boats lay for them; they had rested the night of the 27th at Raipati, being four *coss* from Phaleza, and from Raipati to Chirand were five.

June 29th.—The army proceeded to Ajaibganj; they were discontented for want of provisions the day before: this being a village of the Company's they got some rice; the boats were moored, before the company marched, reinforced by Lieutenant Armstrong with another company of sepoys. We had heard that Nidiram was coming to fight with us with 3,000 horse and 5,000 foot.

June 30th.—Got under way, but made a bad hand of it, the streams being very strong in this river which obliged us to put to the other shore, when we discovered within a mile of us four stands of colours and some horse, which obliged us to put into the stream, and, getting foul of another boat, broke our rudder. We were taken into tow by two guard boats, which, with great labour, brought us to the ground we left in the morning. Here we patched up our rudder as well as we could, and were greatly assisted in it by Mr. Place who came in the pinnace for that purpose. We observed several villages on fire about a *coss* from us, and heard of one Somero, with four or five companies of seapoys and three or four guns, having crossed over hereabouts in order to join Ramnidy, the Phousdar of the country who has got together about 3,000 horse and foot in order to oppose us. We tracked up to the fleet with great danger and difficulty, for we had nearly overset two or three times. When we joined them, had the agreeable news of our having defeated Ramnidy that morning, and killed about 200 of his people. About evening, had an account of Somero's having joined him, and their having encamped within a *coss* of our troops. The place we now lay at is an island, opposite the upper end of which our people are now encamped, but the stream is too strong for us to be able to get round to them. Therefore, having informed Mr. Ellis of it, we are ordered to proceed to the lower end in the morning, when they will march down to us. About 400 men horse and foot are on the opposite shore attending our motions, but they have only one boat.

were wounded in the fray came to us, which made us very anxious about them, as they had both our treasure and our ammunition; but, notwithstanding, we did not endeavour to join them this evening, which proved afterwards very unfortunate.

June 30th.—We had no alarm all night; we marched at 3; scarcely could find anybody to be our guide, as our chief *harcaras* and servants had mostly left us; our intention was to get at our boats. We crossed a *nulla* which was betwixt us and the river Dowie and marched betwixt them. About 7 o'clock we spy'd, about a *coss* ahead, a stand of red colours, which we took to be some choukee, but upon coming nearer we found there were about 50 men with them. Immediately Captain Tabby's battalion stretched to the right to get betwixt them and the *nulla*, but they took to the *nulla*, and most of them were drowned; two or three we took prisoners, but could learn nothing from them. Here we proposed halting till we brought up our rear, as we were within a *coss* of our intended embarkation; but presently we heard a firing in the rear and upon examining we found the enemy advancing. Immediately the rear got up, and we beat to arms and marched back to meet the enemy; they appeared to be about 2,000 and 200 horse. Our men seemed in good spirits and marched on very eagerly, and on the first onsett the enemy were broke and took to their heels. We pursued them about a *coss* and burnt two small villages in the way to dislodge them in case any were there; they took to the *topes*, and we made a halt. We reckoned that we killed about 200. During our stay, we had intelligence from the boats that the current was so strong, that they could not track up to the place intended; so it was agreed they should come down to the end of the island. It divides the river, Dowie here into two branches, which was almost opposite to us: accordingly that advice was sent them. About 2 in the afternoon, the enemy from the *tope* began to fire upon a party of our seapoys that was in a small *tope* nigh them with a two-pounder, but we imagined it was covering their retreat; but, at about three, we were undeceived, for they began to draw out of

June 30th.—We marched rom Ajaibganj to Manpura, five *coss*. The boats came up within a *coss* of the camp into the Dakwa river, but it was with great difficulty, we being obliged to track. Nidiram came and was defeated, with no loss on our side, but about 200 of his men killed. This day a boat that fell in the rear was taken; a havildar and eight sepoys was in it, three of them were killed, the rest joined, but without their arms. Nidiram went upwards Chupra, a few *coss*, where he met Shimroo with three battalions of sepoys and eight pieces of cannon, and a large body of horse sent from Patna after us. Shimroo made Nidiram return, but we had no intelligence of them: our *harcarahas* had all deserted, and none of the country people would come near us.

the *tope*, and began a pretty brisk cannonade, that we were obliged to call in the party of seapoys that was nigh them, and presently they began to fire from the opposite side of the *nullah*, and a stand of Armenian colours was sett up there, which made us understand that they had been joined by one Sumro (an Armenian) who commanded in the Budgepoore country. We got under arms, and waited to see whether they would advance, but they kept their ground and continued their cannonade most of the afternoon. In the evening Mr. Ellis etc., with the principal officers held a council of war to see what the most prudent step to be taken, the purport of which I understood to be, that we ought to be upon the defensive, as our principal design was to cover our boats, and that it would be time enough to fight when we had them with us; accordingly, it was resolved to keep our ground all night and march at two in the morning to join our boats and embark.

July 1st.—We dropped down and joined the army, and immediately landed our howitz, but before they could get it mounted the enemy appeared, and began a brisk cannonade with three or four pieces of cannon. Our people beat to arms and drew up with $\frac{\text{that part}}{\text{the branch}}$ of the river which forms the island on their left and [took] a pretty high bank, with the great river about 200 yards behind it $\frac{\text{in}}{\text{on}}$ their $\frac{\text{rear}}{\text{right}}$, much as follows. * * * * *
They seemed not inclined to attack us. Therefore our people all settled down in order to be more safe from the cannonade, which was brisk. About 8 o'clock Mr. Ellis and all the civil gentlemen, except Lushington, came over to the island to the boats, which began soon after to transport over the baggage by which means great numbers of the seapoys stole over and concealed themselves in the jungle. The enemy seeing their fire did little effect us, slackened it much; however, about eleven, an unlucky shot hit Captain Carstairs as he was sitting down. It entered the inside of his thigh and passed out at his $\frac{\text{loins}}{\text{groin}}$. From the nature of it, it must be mortal. All the day after we had only two or three seapoys killed and

July 1st.—At two we marched, stretching down the side of the river till we came to the end of the island, and halted. At break of day, we saw some of our boats coming round the island; it was agreed to embark the seapoy women and baggage first to the island. About six we spy'd the enemy marching out of the *tope*, making their front towards us: (the *nullah* was then betwixt us and them). Our embarkation began about seven, and to our great surprise found numbers of seapoys wanted to go off with the baggage, and with great difficulty could restrain them: presently the enemy began to cannonade, and kept up a very brisk one with at least five or six pieces of cannon, but did no mischief the first two hours. We got our howitt ashore, which was in one of the boats, and about thirty rounds of grape. Our resolution was to keep our ground on the bank of the river till evening, and if they advanced, then to give them a brisk attack, as we had not ammunition to risk two attacks. About ten, our Chief thought he was of no use on the side of the river that the cannonade was; accordingly he set off for the island and his Fourth in Council about an hour before him. I and some of the civilians soon followed

July 1st.—The army came to the banks of the Dahwa, across from where they lay at Manpore; the Dahwa formed three streams at this place, our boats got into the middle one, and could not pass through for want of water; they were half a mile from the army and were ordered down to the place where the three streams met; the army likewise moved this morning and in marching off, the picket of 100 sepoys lost their way and had a warm scuffle with part of Shimroo's guards. Only the Subahdar and 35 sepoys with the colours got to us. About 8 o'clock we were surrounded by Shimroo with three battalions of sepoys, eight pieces of cannons, a body of about 10,000 horse and foot, Nidiram included: two of Shimroo's battalions had Europe arms, and one country matchlocks. On their approach orders were sent for the 200 sepoys (that had been left to guard the boats) to join us. We got the howitzer landed and prepared to receive them; they came within 800 yards and began to cannonade us. There was a *nullah* about 500 yards in our part, but little water in it and a small bank in front of our line, behind which we were drawn up. The enemy did not seem much inclinable to attack us, but kept a brisk fire from their artillery and jinjalls. About 10 o'clock, it

as many wounded. Mr. Ellis had resolved, if possible, to attack the enemy in the evening, and so to cross to the island, and thence to the budgero/bhajuri side, where we had not above a *coss* to march out of the Province. In the evening it was thought by Captain Tabby, who commanded, and most of the other officers, that it would be very impracticable to attack the enemy in their present disposition, more especially as they found they had lost one third of their seapoys, so that their present force could not exceed $\frac{300}{700}$ sepoys, with the Europeans, which were about 180, including the artillery. While they were deliberating on the matter, they were alarmed by the enemy being in motion and advancing on them We beat . The party of the enemy or the right marched and joined the main body who advanced and kept firing from at the artillery. when they came within a proper distance, Turner's battalion gave their fire [regularly but we could not observe any regular fire] from the right, only a universal popping. Some few European Platomry fired, and then on a grape coming amongst them, they went to the right about, which threw everything into the utmost confusion, and everybody sought their safety in flight. Some swam to the island, and brought us the melancholy news. The boat-people were terrified by the numbers who came pressing on them, and put off to a small distance having on board Captain Carstairs, Captain Wilson, Dr. Campbell and myself, Ensign Armstrong and McKay, who has swam to the island to come off to us with two soldiers, and some five or six gentleman's servants and three or four seapoys, six women, six children. In this confusion we observed many boats going off and knew not what to do for the best. To escape was impossible, therefore we resolved as we were already sufficiently full of people to proceed down to Patna, if possible, and so to surrender ourselves prisoners to the Subah. Accordingly, we put off, and on passing the jungle, which was in the rear of our army, were hailed and fired at two or three times, but could not think of going to the shore, else the crowds would certainly have sunk the boat. We rowed down as softly as possible in order to avoid the Chief. About eleven we had the disagreeable news of poor Carstairs being mortally wounded; he was soon afterwards brought over, and upon dressing him, I found the wound to be mortal; he was brought aboard Captain Wilson's budgeroo and begged of me that I would not leave him. The enemy kept advancing slowly towards us, keeping up at the same time a brisk cannonade; wounded a few of our people. We mustered about a hundred seapoys upon the island and sent over to them, and remained on our ground. About six in the evening, the enemy had come across the *nullah*, almost within random shot, and, about an hour afterwards, came to engage our left wing which was composed of Captain Turner's battalion, and they gave them a very warm reception, which gave us a great expectation that so soon as they engaged our Europeans they would soon be broke; but we were greatly alarmed to find that there was no regular fire afterwards, and presently were informed by some officers and Europeans that swarm over that we were entirely routed. Captain Wilson and us that were in the budgro thought it prudent to haul off from the shore, as it was impossible to keep the seapoys and rabble from filling the boat, which we accordingly did, and afterwards thought we could be of no further service; wherefore we resolved to proceed down the river, and deliver ourselves up, as we had got aboard as many people as our boat could well carry, and immediately set out, having aboard eight Europeans, a number of seapoy women and seapoys: met with no interruption all night, but very dismal thoughts.

was determined that we should attack them; and Mr. Ellis, being much fatigued and somewhat out of order, came down to the boats and ordered some liquor to be sent up to the men. A little after this, Captain Carstairs was mortally wounded with a jinjall ball, and the command devolved on Captain Tabby. Our people were not allowed to fire on account of the great scarcity of ammunition; and the enemy began to come near and nearer, but very slowly. At three in the afternoon, a company of their sepoys came down to the banks of the *nullah* and lay behind them and kept a warm fire of musketry on us; they all after this moved down by degrees and used to stop the cannon and fire and then moved again. Our troops were much fatigued for want of provisions, etc., and being exposed to a warm fire all day. About half an hour after sunset, the firing increased and they began to ply us with musketry crossed the *nullah* and attacked us on all sides. About 8 o'clock at night, the Europeans broke and fled; the sepoys stood their ground, keeping a warm fire upon the enemy till all their ammunition was expended when they likewise gave way. Lieutenants Pickering and Crofts, both of the sepoys were killed, and the rest of the gentlemen that were in the field were taken either that night or next morning. The boat where Mr Ellis was, finding the fire cease, and some of the officers, that could swim, crossed the branch of the river (for the boats lay on an island) opposite to where the action was, pushed off, and got into the river. Messrs. Ellis, Howitt and Smith with Captain Joecher, thought proper to write to Nidiram to send some of his people to conduct them to Patna to Mindialy Cawn, and it was likewise determined that Mr. Ellis should write to Mindialy Cawn desiring that he should send orders for conducting him and the gentlemen safe there. About ten at night, I was sent with a letter to Mindialy Cawn in a small *dingee*, alarming the *chokeys* which are pretty many on this river. We were often hailed, but made no answer, We cut our mast down in order to disfigure the boat, and procured *jumahs* and *turbands* for as many of us as we could, threw many things overboard, lest they should betray who we were, no swords, belts, sashes, etc., and thus spent a melancholy night with poor Carstairs and all of us in the cabin, with women and children, and every moment expecting to be stopped by *chokeys* who might have found an interest to have murdered us all for the sake of plunder, for we had about Rs. 20,000 of the Company's on board. Near to Mineer/Maner, as we imagined it to be, our boat ran aground which perplexed us much, and a boat had kept us company for an hour which we suspected much. In short, we were wavering whether to go ashore or not and take our fate by land, but could not think of leaving Carstairs, whothough mortally wounded, was perfectly sensible. It must have added to his uneasiness to have his friends leave him helpless in such distress. However, while we were aground, we lost sight of the boat that accompanied us, and having got off and into the proper channel, we proceeded down, till about dawn of day, when we were met by a Jemidar on an elephant.

July 2nd.—With about 100 attendants, who were marching up, they hai'd us, and desired us to stop. We told them we were a Dutch *budgero* from Chupra. We not stopping they fired on us, and, I believe, we would have come to, had it not been for a boy of Captain Turner's who told us it was the best to proceed on till we were stopped by force and then tell them we were going to the Subah, which we thought very just. By brisk rowing we got clear of these people without anybody being hurt, and were not troubled any more, except a small boat with three Moors who came aboard and told us they were a *chokey.* We desired them to take us to Patna, but they seemed better pleased that we should give them *buxies*, so we give them twenty rupees and they left us. When we drew near to the Sinjia/Mahi river, we judged it would be better to go to

July 2nd.—Before break of day, we were at a great loss whether we should not go ashore before daylight, as we thought there was a greater probability of meeting the people more humane some distance from the river; but a boy of Captain Turner's said that we had best proceed down the river as far as we could, and if we met with any interruption we had only to say we were going to the Nabob, which advice we thought very prudent, and accordingly pursued it. We met no interruption till about 7 o'clock, when a boat boarded us; by giving them Rs. 30 and acquainting them we were going to the Nabob, they went off. About eight, a party of seapoys going up the river hailed us, and fired a shot or two at us, but we proceeded on, and they left us; we then resolved to go to Hadgipoor, and deliver ourselves up to the Phousdar (being a relation of Mir

July 2nd.—And got down to Patna, about twelve next morning, the 2nd July. I sent immediately to the Nabob to let him know what I was come for; he sent for me, and used me very well, sending an order to Nidiram to conduct the gentlemen safe to him; but before that could arrive they were all taken by Shimroo that morning. About ten I was kept close prisoner in the killa, and at night the Naib came and desired me to write a chit to some gentlemen that were come in a *budgero* to Hajipore to come to him, as they might be ill-used by the country people, which I did. They came two days after, and were immediately sent to Mongheer, but were sent back again and kept in the Chahalsatun. They had buried Captain Carstairs, who died of his wounds in his *budgero.* These gentlemen were Captain Wilson, Lieutenant Armstrong, Ensign Mackay, Mr.

Hadgipore, and surrender ourselves, as we might meet with milder / should meet with better treatment there than from the people of Patna, who were highly incensed. Besides Phousdar, being a brother of Meer Abdoula's, might use us better on that account. We put about. [About noon, we arrived at Hadgipore, and were very kindly received by the Phousdar's son.]

Sunday, July 3rd.—Poor Carstairs died on shore at a small house that had been provided for him. We had a coffin made, and had him buried as decently as circumstances would allow. The same day had a *chit* from Doctor Fullerton, who desired us to come over to Patna, told us we would meet with a gentle usage from the Subah.

Monday, July 4th.—Had our effects taken account of, and were to be sent to Patna next day. Our treatment here is very easy, having several provisions sent us from the Phousdar, but find our guards and his servants very troublesome for *buxies*, which we find best to satisfy. Heard from the Phousdar that our army had marched, that Mr. Amyatt had gone down, but Mr. Hay and another gentleman still continued at Mongheer.

Tuesday, July 5th.—Our Phousdar with our guard accompanied us over to Patna. We landed at the *Killa*, and were brought to the Durbar, when we were kindly received by Ally Minde Cawn, and had victuals brought us in plenty, after giving us *betel*. We were shewn to our apartment under the care of Mirza Caleil, a near

Abdulla's), thinking the populace at Patna might be too much *irritated* still, and not so safe for us; accordingly we arrived at Hadgipoor river. About twelve sent a servant ashore to the Phousdar to acquaint him we were come to deliver ourselves up; he soon returned with some of the principal people, and acquainted us that the Phousdar was then at Patna, but he had a son, who acted in his absence. We were conducted very civily by these people to him, and he received us very kindly, after taking our leave, sent us refreshment. Carstairs continues to grow worse every hour.

July 3rd.—The Phousdar arrived from Patna last night; sent for Captain Wilson; continues to behave himself kindly; sent a standing cot for Captain Carstairs, and appointed a house for his being ashore, as his wounds began to mortify and very offensive to us in the boat; prevailed upon him to go ashore about 12; at 3 he died. We applied for a coffin and *bildaars* to make a grave; they were soon furnished, and we interred the corpse about 6, in the most decent manner we could. This evening we received a *chitt* from Fullerton, who had delivered himself up to the Nabob at Patna; he acquainted us that he was most genteely treated, and advised us to come over. We was then informed by the Phousdar that there was an order for going to Patna, which was agreeable to us.

July 4th.—This morning we were in great expectations of the Phousdar's coming to carry us to Patna, but we heard nothing of him till about 3, when his son arrived to take an inventory of all our *chœsbaz*. We were a little uneasy to find we did not go to Patna this evening, but we were assured that he would be with us int he morning to carry us over.

July 5th.—At 8, the Phousdar came down and sett off with us. We arrived about 11 opposite to our factory, when we were hailed by the seapoys to bring to; there the Phousdar asked us whether we choosed to go (Marcott, an Armenian, commanded them), but we insisted on going to the Nabob; it seems they are obliged to carry us to the highest

Anderson, Surgeon and Mr. Peter Campbell, and two soldiers.

relation of his own, who, for the short time we remained with him, did his utmost to render everything as agreeable as possible to us (even menial services). He sent for us to his own room, and had some country spirit for us to drink of, gave orders to bring all our things, and that there must not be the least thing touched. We thought ourselves extremely happy in such gentle usage, for the Nabob himself came and sat down with us at Mirza Caleil's, and told us he expected Mr. Ellis with 30 gentlemen and 120 sepoys the next day, for they had set out from Chupra. At 9 we returned to our apartment, when Mr. Fullerton came an hour after, and acquainted us that orders had come sending us to Mongheer, that we must go immediately. This surprised us much as it was very dark and the stream rapid, but by speaking to our friend Mirza Caleil, it was put off till the morning. Accordingly, early we got all ready, and had our things sent to the *budgero* where he went himself to see us safe delivered ~~safe and to deliver us~~ to the jamidar who had charge of us. He had sent some bread and a roasted kid into the boat for our use which we took very kind. Captain Wilson with great difficulty persuaded him to accept of his sword in a compliment.

In command if we choose it; the Phousdar left it to our choice. Accordingly, we proceeded, and soon after our arrival, were brought up from the boats, guarded by a party of seapoys, to the Durbar in the *Killa*; was very gently received by the Governor. Upon breaking up of the Durbar, had a very good dinner served us up; presently afterwards was shown to our apartments, which were under the care of a near relation of the Governor, who entertained us in the most obliging, complaisant manner imaginable; the most minute necessary that we might want he did not forgett. In the evening he invited us to his own apartment, and treated us with very good arrack and a *hooka*. Just before supper, we were informed that an order was arrived for our setting out for Mongheer, and we was ordered to get ourselves in readiness to sett off directly, which gave us great uneasiness, as we were very fatigued, but by the intercession of our friend who kept us, it was put off till the morning.

Wednesday, July 6th.—On the morning we put off with two guard boats and some seapoys with us in the *budgero*, which had not got out of sight of the Killa, when the boats were lashed alongside the better to secure us, and so we drove down like a log, but they soon found it inconvenient as well as we, and cast loose, one going ahead, the other astern of us, and thus we went on till we got to Barr, where we halted for the night. Our guard were so careful of us to-night as to keep all the cabin windows fast by running a rope quite round them.

Thursday, July 7th.—Early we got under way, and proceeded down to Nabob gunge, where we made a hearty meal of *cutchere* and a dram of country arrack our friend at Hadgipore had given us.

July 6th.—About 6 o'clock, our things were sent into the boats, and as we set off about 7 in our *budgero* and two guard boats with 50 gun men were conducted to the water side by our friend. At first setting off, our guard seemed as if they would be very troublesome by lashing their boats on each side of our *budgero* and fastening the windows; the Governor sent us a dressed kid, bread, etc., for our voyage. We reached this evening at Barr.

July 7th.—Sett off at break of day. Our guard was more complaisant than before; our entertainment to-day was rice, dall, and ghee, which they say makes a very good *cutcheree*. We reached this evening Nabob gunge; our guard hauls alongside of us and shuts our windows.

July 6th.—Mr. Ellis with the rest of the gentlemen were brought to Patna. I petitioned the Nabob to be sent to them, or be suffered to see them both of which were refused.

Friday, July 8th.—Cast loose and proceeded to Mongheer, which makes no bad appearance from the river, where you have a front view of the palace His Excellency has lately built there with a breast-work before it for 30 guns. It began to rain and blow about 12, by which means we drove past it, and were obliged to track up about a mile, and at 5 arrived at the gate close to the lower part of the Fort. Our *harcarrah* went on shore with the letter, but had nobody came to us but a rascal of a German who had been formerly in our service; he pretended to have come from the Nabob to know our number, names, and nation.

Saturaay, July 9th.—As nobody has come to-day to inquire whether we want victuals, nor even our own *harcarrah* returned, it is a matter of surprise to our guards as well as ourselves. We send to the bazar for what we want in the eating way, having money to the amount of 800 rupees.

Sunday, July 10th.—Aservant of Mr. Place's brought us a chit giving us an account of how Messrs. Johnstone and Harris, with two Europeans more belonging to the boats with arms, being close prisoners, and having only ½ a sir of coarse rice per day each for their subsistence; that they were in want of some clothes, which they beg us to send if we could spare. They mentioned also their having 10 rupees each given them two days before to buy meat, etc. They had surrendered themselves at Patna to Mr. Marcott, who finding them merchants, gave them leave to go down if they could, but they found it impossible to pass the *chokie* boats at Mongheer, which are placed on both sides of the river pretty close, besides every sand in the middle of the river has one or two: all of them have one or two seapoys. As the servant who brought the chit had a seapoy with him, and our guard would scarce permit him to come back into the boat, we found it impossible to send them clothes. We therefore put up 28 rupees, and wrote a chit giving an account of our situation, etc., but they kept so good a look-out, that we could find no opportunity of sending it. Three Armenians came into / on board to us who gave us news of our army being

July 8th.—Sett off early as usual; got in sight of Mongheer about 10, abreast of the Fort at 12, but a squall coming off sett us past it, so that we could not track up again till 5; was in expectation of some officer to come and examine us, but to our surprise nobody enquired after us, but a durty scoundrel of a German, a deserter from us, which curiosity had induced him to come and see who we were; this evening my servant (named Nimmo) ran away with Rupees 30 of mine, some combs, etc.

July 9th.—All this day, to our great surprise, we heard nothing from the Nabob, nor any of his officers, which we could not comprehend the reason of. We furnished ourselves with provisions etc., from the bazar.

July 10th.—Still lying in our *budgero*: in the afternoon our boy from the bazar acquaints us that the *harcara* told him that he had got the Nabob's perwannah for our returning to Patna; in the evening it was confirmed.

July 8th.—Mr. Ellis with the rest of the gentlemen were sent to Mongheer and there confined; there was 45,000 of the Company's cash on board the *budgero* when Mr. Ellis was taken and some plate which was given to him. but in the care of some of the Nabob's people to be given him when he wanted it; some time it remained with Khwaj Petrus, afterwards with Mindialy Cawn.

at Cutwa. We wanted them to deliver the money to Johnsone, etc., but they declined it, as they were strangers, and had only come to trade. At night we had an account from our *harcarrah* that we were to return to Patna, and he was providing *dandies* for that purpose.

Monday, July 11th.—The *harcarrah* got the perwannah for our going, but could not procure *dandies*. The Jamidar of our guard sent and pressed about a dozen in the evening, so could not set off till to-morrow. Within these two days, a large boat or two has brought to this ghat, our two 24-pounders with carriage, guns and transport carriages with which they carried them off.

Tuesday, July 12th.—We set out in our way to Patna with a fair wind but strong stream. Afternoon, about 4 *coss* from Mongheer, we passed Marcott's encampment with a party of sepoys, who are going to Mongheer. Heard that Captain Turner and two other officers came down with him, and had gone to Mongheer. We stopped a *coss* above them.

Wednesday, July 13th.—Got early under way, and at Nabob gunge met about five or six companies of seapoys with two pieces of cannon and a few horse and 90 of our Europeans, who had taken service, but gave us to understand it was to avoid bad usage, and with a view to making their escape. They told us Mr. Ellis and all the other gentlemen had gone down to Mongheer excepting Lieutenant Pickering and Ensign Crofts, who were either killed or drowned on the 1st We crossed the river and sailed up to a large island, when getting where on ground, obliged us to

July 11th.—This morning no appearance of our setting off, which surprised us. In the afternoon we received a chit from Harris and Johnstone acquainting us that they were confined in the Fort in a durty house, and very indifferently treated; allowed half a seer of rice per man a day. We endeavoured to write them an answer, and send them some money, but could not find their servant afterwards. About 7, the *harcarrah* arrives with five or six *dandies* or rather cooleys, to carry us up, but our Jamedar sent one of his people and pressed about a dozen of tolerable *dandys*.

July 12th.—Upon getting up this morning, I was greatly alarmed with a violent pain in my instep of my foot; could attribute no cause for it, unless it was Dr. Anderson's head, who lay just by my feet; as it is pretty heavy, it was generally believed to be the cause by lying on it. About 10, our *dandys* were all on board, and we sett off; got up by evening about six *coss*; the pain of my instep increased to a violent degree, and before evening was fully satisfied that it was not owing to Dr. Anderson's head but rather appeared to be a touch of gout, which I am very sorry for.

July 13th.—We got under way early; reached within a *coss* of Rua Nalda; by evening the violent pain on my foot still continues, which puts it past all doubt that it is the gout; spoke to some of our soldiers, who are marching down, and have taken service with the Nabob; they informed us that 100 and upwards had taken service; they also informed us that Mr. Ellis and all the officers were sent down to Mongheer, which surprises us the more that we are sent up again; they say also there were only two officers killed Ensigns, Pickering and Crofts.

stop for the night about a *coss* below Ruinalla on the opposite shore.

Thursday, July 14th.—Not finding water for us within the island, and the current being too strong without it, we crossed the river again, by which we drove a *coss* back, and had great danger, and difficulty in tracking up to Ruinalla as the stream was very strong, and the banks fell in pretty freqent. In passing the *nulla*, we observed three flag-elephants with about 2,000 horse and foot crossing in boats on their way to Mongheer. In the afternoon, being within a large island, we had a fair wind and smooth water, which ran us within 2 *coss* of Derriapur, where we were brought to for the night.

Friday, July 15th.—We proceeded up tracking as there was little wind. At 11 o'clock we stopped at Derriapur to dress our victuals; in the meantime three companies of seapoys, mostly our own, who had taken service, arrived here on their way down. At one o'clock, we put off with a pretty breeze, and at sunset reached Mohura, about 2 *coss* below Ponnerac.

Saturday, July 16th.—Early we got under way with a fair wind, about........we passed Ponnerac, at 12 we stopped at Bar to dress victuals. Here were a large body of horse and seapoys encamped with most of our tents, etc., in their charge. Their route is for Mongheer. At 2, we put off, and went a *coss* further.

Sunday, July 17th.—We set out early with a brisk wind, which continuing all day, brought us within a mile of Jaffier Khan's garden at sunset.

Monday, July 18th.—Got under way at 5, and arrived at the Killa at about 9, when, after waiting two hours we were ordered to the Diwan, as the Nabob was not at home, who ordered dinner for us. Here we remained pestered with flies and heat till about 8 o'clock, when we were sent for by the Nabob, who, as before, received us very kindly, ordered chairs for us to sit on, gave a *hooka* to Captain Wilson, and told us not to be uneasy, for we might look on ourselves at

July 14th.—Nothing remarkable to-day; we advanced about 5 *coss*; numbers of the Nabob's seapoys and troops on the road going down, also several of ours taken service.

July 15th.—Got under way early; advanced by evening as far as Moor, within 2 *coss* of Ponnerac; my foot a good deal easier; nothing remarkable; a scarcity of provisions.

July 16th.—Got under way as usual; advanced by evening as far as Barr. We feasted to-day on rice, dall and ghee.

July 17th.—Nothing remarkable all this day; had a fine breeze; advanced by evening within a *coss* of Jaffier Khan's garden.

July 18th.—Arrived at Patna by 10: soon afterwards Captain Willson was sent for ashore. About 12, we were all sent for; understood that the Governor was at the west gate. We were received by the Dewan; were kept in a sort of Durbar place, immensely close and hott; had dinner brought us. The Governor did not come in till about 6; an hour afterwards he sent for us, received us very politely, and made us understand we should have every indulgence in his power. He

July 16th.—I was sent down to Mongheer and there confined separately from the rest of the gentlemen. As I afterwards understood, they were all well used, though strictly confined. We had victuals sent us by the Nabob regularly once a day.

home, that he would provide a proper place for us in a few days, as that we were in was very hot we should sleep in a bungalo above stairs. We took our leave, and thought oursleves very happy in falling into so good hands. The bungalo was the Dewan's sleeping place : it was cleared accordingly, and we were ordered up from our hot apartment where we regaled ourselves with the refreshing breeze till near 11. Soon after our supper came, which we paid little regard to, it being so late. Our guard, consisting of 20 *bergundassies* and 5 seapoys slept on the terrace, while we crept into the bungalo where, we found but little rest, as it was swarming with bugs and mosquito es.

Tuesday, July 19th.—At daylight we were roused out, and returned to our hot room. Our Gentoo friend, the Dewan, I believe, was not well pleased at our sleeping within, for he ordered mats and carpets to be taken off and washed, and took possession himself, giving us his *dewancanah* to ourselves, except a small part divided by a *purda* for his cook-room, and at noon they began to cook there, which filled our apartment with smoke, which with the heat and flies we were sufficiently tormented. We made a complaint of it, and have a promise of its being removed. To-day our boy brought in a few bottles of liquor which were seized by the guards as they must have the Nabob's *perwannah* for it to pass in. At night the Nabob's *consamah* came to inform us that he had his master's orders for whatever we chose to have dressed, and we need only send to the cookroom for it. To-night we found it very disagreeable on account of heat, bugs, and a noisy guard who occupy the verando of our house.

Wednesday, July 20th.—Nothing extraordinary, only a visit from Mirza Caleil, who tells us that he is going to Mongheer. To-night the Dewan ordered the guard to sleep out that we might have the verando to sleep in, which was a great piece of service to us. We had a little air, and less noise.

assured us that we should have a more airy and retired apartment than what we were in at present, and provided us with the Dewan's bungalo for the night, which was very cool and pleasant ; he at the same time acquainted us, he believed the reason of our being sent up here again was owing to the letter he wrote to the Nabob, wherein he mentioned to him if he had not conveniency at Mongheer, he begged he would return us to him.

July 19th.—Early in the morning we were brought down from the bungalo to our old apartment, for as we were in hourly expectation of our being removed to a proper place allotted to us, we thought nothing of it. About 10, in one end of the room where we was, a fire was lighted, which had almost suffocated us with heat and smoke ; it was to dress the Dewan's victuals ; as he is a Gentoo, he can't dress in any of the Moorman's cook-rooms. Upon our complaining, they assured us it should be done no more. We passed this day very disagreeably, no order for bringing our things from the *budgero*, nor any other place appointed us ; the cause we understood to be the Dewan's being affronted at our laying in his bungalo last night. We got a few bottles of wine from the Dutch Factory, but our guard understanding it, insisted upon seizing them, which they did accordingly to the great mortification of some of our mess mates. We found we could have no admittance to the Governor this night, and resolved to bear everything patiently.

July 20th.—We passed a very disagreeable night from the intense heat, but we comforted ourselves that we should be removed soon ; passed the day as before, but to our surprise no order for our removal ; can't divine the cause ; resolved to bear everything with patience till we can see the Governor. In the evening our Jimidar told us we might lay down in the yard if it was too

Thursday, July 21st.—Nothing remarkable

Friday, July 22nd.—In the afternoon, about 4, we were on a sudden removed from our quarters, leaving two soldiers. We were led into the city, and on our way met two Europeans with a guard who told us there were 15 of them come up from Mongheer. We were led through several windings and by-ways to a place where all sorts of prisoners are confined, and, after passing two compounds, we came to a third where we observed, some prisoners in irons, which gave us but and indifferent idea of the place, more especially as the apartment we were put into was quite close damp, and hung with cobwebs. [Some mats were in the part close to] the door which were [secured and] tied down, so that what light and air we had was from the door. Here, to all appearances, we had reason to expect but indifferent treatment, but we had not been here an hour before we began to be somewhat better reconciled to it, for all our things were sent to us very carefully. We found this a place for state prisoners, and several people of some consequence had been here since Ramnarain's misfortunes. There is about 200 peons as a guard to this prison, who allow us to walk all the length of the square, so that we are here more retired and have more liberty.

hot; we choosed the verando if he would move his guard from hence, which was done. We had a far more agreeable night than the former: our guard consisted of a Jimidar, about 20 gunmen and two seapoys with sword and bayonet.

July 21st.—We passed the last night more comfortable than the former, as it was tolerable cool, and not so much pestered with bugg. We now gave over expectations of seeing the Governor, and were satisfied we should have no remove; got a pack of cards, and amused ourselves with a game at whist; much troubled with flies, and the time hangs very heavy. We are to lay in the verando as before; had all our baggage from the *budgero*, and find that our boys have stolen 138 Rupees; are afraid to deliver them up to justice, upon account of our transaction at the Hadgipore; allowed two of them to go away, whom we judge to be guilty.

July 22nd.—Passed the night tolerably well: find it impossible to be allowed any wine or spirits; they kept five bottles in their possession which we got the first day from the Dutch Factory. About 4 in the afternoon we were acquainted that we were to be removed to another place, and immediately orders came for our removal, which was very agreeable to us. We all sett out, and were much surprised when they brought us out of the *Killah* through the street, a spectacle to the whole populace, about the distance of half a mile; landed us at last in a square, where the first objects that presented us were two or three in irons, in our situation no agreeable sight to be sure. We were shown our room, which had been a storehouse and cleared out this day for our reception, full of rats and the floor dug or burrowed with fifty of their holes. I retired into it, and layed myself down in one of the corners to be free from the gazing of our new companions who were in irons, and found a small window where I could peep through, and contemplated upon our sad situation; began to wish we were in our old apartments again, but at last concluded that everything was for the best (in this best of possible worlds, as Mr. Candide observes,) and so comforted ourselves; presently

Saturday, July 23rd.—We had a visit from Ramnarain's Catwal, a man of good character and formerly of great influence in the city. We had no victuals sent us, so we are obliged to furnish ourselves. We heard to-day that on the 15th instant a body of our troops had an engagement at Catwa with the force from Maxadavad, and the latter entirely defeated, the two principal jemidars being killed. That Houghly we have taken and destroyed. Our gentlemen at Cassimbazar had sent off their valuable effects, and theirselves got safe off. That the Nabob was preparing to go down.

Sunday, July 24th.—To-day we were a good deal alarmed by some of our guards having a parcel of old irons, which we imagined were intended for us, but it was only to move them to another place. All of our servants were ordered to sleep out of the square, except one.

Monday, July 25th.—Our boys heard a rumour today in the Dutch Factory of Mr. Amyatt and his brother-in-law being both killed in their passage down near Rajahmaul, having made resistance to a force ordered to stop them, but we cannot give

our *chizbuss* arrives, and to our great comfort, none of our guards as they had turned very impudent and disagreeable. We found this place to be the prison for state prisoners, and that there was confined here Ramnarain's family and all his dependents, which was some relief to find our companions were no worse sort of people. We had the liberty to walk about in the square without anybody attending us and find ourselves much more retired than before, as our guard here are principally stationed at the gates. We were now sensible that the fine speeches the Governor made us were from motives of true Eastern policy.

July 23rd.—We had a very agreeable night and begin to like our prison much better than our former apartments; passed the day very agreeably; sent out and purchased victuals for ourselves; sent in the evening to the *Killa* to know whether we were to expect entertainments from hence or not; were given understand that we must provide ourselves in everything we wanted; have visits from some of our fellow prisioners, who we find to be very sensible men, and who condole with us in our present situation.

July 24th.—Had a pleasant night, and find our new habitation quite retired and as agreeable as we could expect; have employed tailors to make us some banyan, shirts, etc., had a leg of roast mutton, and currie, steaks, etc., for dinner, and a draught of good cool *sherbitt* to wash it down: we were a little alarmed about 5 with our keeper and guard taking out four or five irons, thinking that they might be for our use, as he gave us a small hint the night before in a joke how we should like them; but we soon found they were only examining them to see if they were in good order.

July 25th.—Passed the night as usual; nothing remarkable to-day further than that our man Nicolo smuggled a bottle of Dutch liquor, which was very acceptable; he got in also this evening two bottles of gin.

credit. Finding the want of liquor, our boys smuggled a bottle which gave us a glass each after dinner and at bed time.

Tuesday, July 26th.—To-day close and sultry, which makes the flies very troublesome to us. Had a small recruit of two bottles of gin, which is two days allowance. The economy we have established is to drink twice a day, dinner at one, talk a while in the evening, and sleep at ten. Supper we have none. The intervals are filled up with reading, gaming, and conversation with our fellow prisoners.

Wednesday, July 27th.—Nothing extraordinary.

Thursday, July 28th.—Our Jamidar inform sus the Nabob has ordered us to send for our provisions to his cookroom as usual. To-day we heard that Mr. Ellis' munshi had got safe to Benares, also that the King and Shuja Dowla are come down to Allahabad.

Friday, July 29th.— On sending to-day for our victuals, the *Cunsamah* said he had not his master's orders, by which means we were disappointed of our dinner.

Saturday, 30th July.—To-day we sent our servants to the Nabob to request that we might be allowed to send to the Dutch for a little liquor daily, as custom had rendered it necessary for our health, also that we might have a daily allowance in money rather than his victuals, as it was not dressed in our way, both of which he granted, allowing us 4 rupees per day and liberty to bring in two bottles of liquor per day.

July 26th.—Nothing remarkable to-day.

July 27th.—Passed our time as usual; Nicolo continues to smuggle a little gin successfully.

July 28th.—To-day we were informed by our Jemidar that he had orders for us to send our boys to the Governor for victuals; nothing remarkable.

July 29th.—Early one of our boys went to the Governor for breakfast, but was told there were no orders. We did not provide anything for dinner, expecting orders would be given by that time, but to our great disappointment we found our mistake, and was obliged to send out to the bazar for what we could get; dined about 4; we despatched a letter down to the Governor, or Commanding Officer.

July 30th.—We resolved to send Mr. Nicolo to the Durbar to the Governor; accordingly he set out without our Jemidar, and acquainted him we should be glad he would order us an allowance in money for victualling ourselves, and he granted us rupees 4 per day; likewise we demanded leave for some liquor; he allowed us to purchase and use two or three bottles per day; we are to sign a daily receipt for our money. We had intelligence a few days ago of our army being at Catwa, and of having had an engagement with the troops belonging to Muxadabad, and had; gained a compleat victory, having killed several of their principal Jemidars.

Sunday, 31st July.—Had a case bottle of gin brought in with authority (having) procured a case from the Dutch Doctor for 50 rupees rather than give two rupees a common bottle, which runs ten wine glasses, while a case bottle runs 30, but we find it much adulterated, which considering the Jew we bought it of, is no surprise. Heard a rumour of our troops being defeated at Plassey

Monday, 1st August.—Heard with pleasure the news of yesterday's reverse, for, from authority, we have gained a second victory over the troops at Muxadabad, and Mr. Morcott with a large body of seapoys, etc., now is (8 *coss*) on this side of the city, so that we may soon hear of an action of consequence, as our whole forces are pretty near them. The Nabob has encamped at Mongheer, near the hot wells, but no appearance of moving yet.

Tuesday, 2nd August.—Had the news of yesterday confirmed, great commotions at Mongheer, and

July 31st.—Very heavy rains for these two days. Our former cook has left us, which would have distressed us much, had it not been for Ensign McKey, who has a thorough knowledge in cookery, and has officiated in that office, greatly to our satisfaction, for these two days. We have provided ourselves with another cook. Don Nicolo purchased a case of gin from the Dutch Snout's Scraper for rupees 50. We propose bringing in two or three bottles at a time according to our allowance, as it comes much cheaper by being bought in quantity; the Snout Scraper being a great Jew, he also sold two knives and forks and two cups and saucers for the small price of rupees 4. Don Nicolo, being a great politician, brought us from the Dutch Factory news that might be depended upon, that our main army has not marched from Calcutta, but that was only a party that was at Cutwa, and that they had a second engagement at Placey with the principal force from Muxadabad, and that the former was only a skrimage with a small party of theirs; that our party was surrounded by numbers of their troops, and every man put to the sword; disagreeable news enough.

August 1st.—Disagreeable conjecture about the situation of our affairs in general, and no very favourable ones about our head managers in particular. A particular friend, who favours us with a little intelligence, informed us to-day that our affairs below went on very prosperously; that our whole force was come up, and that a second encounter had happened near the lower capital, and that we had compleately routed their whole force, having killed in this engagement their principal Commander, and obtained everything; this news we have very good authority for, which oversetts our friend Don Nicolo entirely. Marcott has proceeded down within eight *coss* of the capital. We expect to have news of him very soon. His Excellency keeps post in Mongheer. Qn. whether he will ever go out of it? I hope not till we fetch him: so much for politics.

August 2nd.—This night we were very much disturbed by buggs and much infected with fleas in

Comgar Cawn with all the other Phousdars and Jamedars called in. Bought to-day six bottles of very good Madeira for three rupees per bottle, with one of which we regaled ourselves on our good news.

Wednesday, 3rd August.—Got a table and three chairs for Rs. 15-8, also a large one for Rs 7. Thus we are pretty well equipped for eating and drinking. Gregan Cawn, with the remainder of the force, is gone down, and His Excellency with a few for a bodyguard only remain.

Thursday, August 4th.—Nothing extraordinary, but are in daily expectation of a battle below.

Friday, August 5th.—Nothing extraordinary, but a rumour of a fight at Muxadabad.

Saturday, August 6th.—Mr. Roach's boy arrived from Mongheer, bringing news of Mr. Amyatts' head being brought there some time ago; that Mr. Chambers and some of the Cossimbazar factory are there, also hear that we were thrice repulsed in the attack of the city of Muxadabad, but the fourth attack carried everything; that the old Nabob is declared. Don Nicolo Muskita / Nicolas our servant brings news of Marcott's being defeated, Somero killed with many elephants and Jamidars, that Marcott had gone over to us with 1,000 men; but I can give no credit to it.

Sunday, August 7th.—Nothing extraordinary.

the day. The former news we have confirmed, with the addition that Meer Jaffier being for certain with our army, and that we are in possession of the Capital, and that the Governor of it is since dead of his wounds. We also hear that Marcott has stopped at Suttee and can advance no further.

August 3rd.—Our news is more and more confirmed and that Gongar Cawn is getting out from Mongheer to join Marcott. We daily expect of hearing of a decisive stroke being made. Dr. Anderson was a little out of humour to-day, and did not eat his dinner as usual, owing to a mistake made in describing a house that he and some gentlemen built at Neg—s (that they had built a house without any dimensions); he is nearly related to my countrymen, I believe, for he seems to have established a maxim that it is not right to give up a point.

August 4th.—Nothing material to-day, save Dr. Anderson was highly offended with me at dinner for wanting to drink out of the cup before he had finished what he calls his allowance of gin.

August 5th.—A very fine day, but furnishes nothing remarkable in the public or private way.

August 6th.—No news these two or three days, which makes us very anxious; this being a Saturday, we commemorated the evening with a couple of bottles of *lall.*

August 7th.—Don Nicolo has picked up a piece of intelligence, which we can give little credit to, that our troops have had an engagement with Marcott, the Armenian; that they had gained a complete victory. Somero, one of their Com-

Monday, August 8th.—Mindy Ali Cawn came into our square, and went soon out. He beckoned us not to rise or disturb ourselves, but we heard soon after that he wanted a place to put 20 Europeans, who had just arrived from Mongheer. Heard at night that we had rescued Mol-or and some of the royal family who were prisoners at Dacca and had settled that country.

Tuesday, August 9th.—Had a chit from one Mr. Bennett, Company's factor at Brampore, and also from Mr. Thomson, agent for Mr. McGuire. They were taken prisoners (below) and sent with about 20 common soldiers; are in great distress, wanting every necessary. We sent them Rs. 20 for the present. The Nabob of this place is preparing to set out for Mongheer in a few days. *Harcarrahs* are in constant motion here, transporting families and effects of the merchants out of the city. Troops from the Phousdars are ordered to join at Mongheer, and a bridge building at Ruinalla. The seaths aremade close prisoners, and great commotions among the great at Mongheer. It is said our troops are marching up, and by the latest advices were 15 *coss* from the lowest capital.

Wednesday, August 10th.—Nothing extraordinary.

Thursday, August 11th.—Hear of an action below in which Morcott's army were entirely defeated and several jamidars gone over to Meer Jaffier, but this wants confirmation. Messrs. Bennett and Thomson were to-day brought to us by the Nabob himself. They gave us an account of

manders, killed, and that Marcott has joined us with a thousand men, but this is only bazar *gup*.

August 8th.—The above news still prevails, but no authority still. To-day the Governor stept in here to see if there was room for some of our prisoners that they were sending up from Mongheer: he did not speak to us; they are put in an apartment in the Chelsea Town. They were taken at Cossimbazar; they are 23 in number, all in irons, amongst whom are Mr. Bennett, and one Thompson, who was in Mr. McGuire's employ.

August 9th.—We had a line from Mr. Bennett, acquainting us that he was destitute of every necessary; we sent him Rs. 20: they confirm the news of Mr. Amyatt's being cut off with seven officers. We have a report that His Excellency at the lower capital has been endeavouring to bribe the two Commanders below, and that they have sent him word to send some people of his of consequence and they would treat with him. We are assuredly informed of Jagat Seath being confined close prisoner at Mongheer. Don Nicolo's last news is fully contradicted: our army is said to be 8 *coss* this side Muxadabad. We daily expect to hear something of consequence.

August 10th.—Nothing remarkable to-day

August 11th.—This morning I had a line from the soldiers; they prove to be mostly belonging to the party that Mr. Amyatt had with him; we sent them Rs. 34. Soon afterwards Messrs. Bennett and Thompson were brought here to be confined along with us; they

August 10th.—The Nabob left Mongheer, and the fort was left in charge of Mohamed Cawn; he treated us with the greatest lenity in appearance, and pretended to carry on a treaty with Mr. Ellis, but it was all a sham, for he never was in earnest. I was allowed to see the gentlemen on account of Captain Turner's being ill, who afterwards died of a flux.

Mr. Amyatt and Ensign Cooper being killed at Muxadabad, as follows:—They had embarked all the party and sent the horses, etc., with the syzes by land. Meeting with contrary winds, it was ten days ere they reached Muxadabad, where at once they saw troops drawn up on each side the river with some great guns. They hailed them and desired them to come to, but, not taking notice of them, some of them fired, on which some of our seapoys began to fire also. and killed some body on the shore, on which the great guns and vollies were fired, which obliged them to put to the opposite shore, where was the least fire. Mr. Amyatt, notwithstanding the fire, landed with a pair of pistols. He took the Nabob's perwannah in one hand and held it up to them, and a pistol in the other, and advanced to the top of the bank, when he was shot in the leg, and soon after cut to pieces. Ensign Cooper met the same fate in making resistance, but the other gentlemen they could give no account of, but expect they were sent to Mongheer, with Mr. Chambers and the others from Cossimbazar. They also informed us that Mr. Hay and Mr. Gulston were left at Mongheer, and remain there yet. These gentlemen have suffered greatly, being put in irons and brought up in one boat, and scarce victuals or necessaries to cover them, being in all 27 persons. The Nabob here allows 10 rupees per day to the 17 people left, and an addition of Rs. 2 per day on account of these two gentlemen.

Friday, August 12th.—Last night late we had a confirmation of the action below, but no particulars. Heard that the Nabob's wives, etc., are gone from Mongheer in order to be in safety. Numbers here are sending their families over the river. Mindy Ali Khan set out to-day with 200 Moguls and some seapoys of Mongheer. To-day two padres, who had a few days ago gone from hence to Mongheer, returned on account of the confusion on the roads. They report the Nabob and all his troops are gone too from thence, and it is believed he goes to make his effort. They heard all the prisoners were embarked in the boats, but this is only hearsay.

give us a particular account of Mr. Amyatt, etc., being cut off; the Nabob came along with and behaved very politely; he told us he was to set out for Mongheer soon. We have this day an account that Morcott has met with a complete overthrow, but we are somewhat incredulous of it; but the news is fully general

August 12th.—Last night our old friend was told that he must not sit so often with us; am afraid we shall lose his company; he seems to give credit to the former news; this evening our Jemidar confirmed it, with the additional circumstances of Morcott being killed, and Samroo wounded, also that the Nabob is came out from Mongheer, and is imagined to go down and try his fate once more; his wife and family are on their way here.

Saturday, August 13th.—By certain intelligence we have gained a complete victory over Marcott: taken 9 pieces of cannon. Three jemidars with 1,300 horses and 1,800 sepoys and Europeans went over to us five days ago. Gregan Cawn got the Nabob to march down the remainder of his force, but with great reluctance. All the prisoners are well at Mongheer. His treasure there yet.

Sunday, August 14th.—Heard that the Nabob marched five days ago with about 6,000 men. Comgar Khan has marched to join him with one thousand horse, and 2,000 horse from Battea are on their way for the same purpose.

Monday, August 15th.—Heard melancholy account of Ramnarain and Raj bullub being both cut off, but as yet not confirmed, though both families here are in great distress on that account.

Tuesday, August 16th.—Still the above report prevails strongly in this city, with this addition of the number being eleven in all, amongst whom are Ellis, Lushington, and 3 *harcarahs*, so it is imagined they have been concerned in an illegal correspondence.

Wednesday, August 17th.—Mr. McKay's servant to-day arrived from Mongheer in four days, who says he left all our gentlemen well there; that Ramnarain, Rajah Raj Bullab and the Seaths were said to be cut off there. Hear our troops are between the passes. His Excellency at Baugle-pore and the bulk of the army at the second pass. The Begum is said to be delivered of a child at Ruinalla, which retards her journey. She has many boats and elephants with 13,000 horse, under command of Nobit Roy. It is said all his money from Mongheer is there.

Thursday, August 18th.—About 500 sepoys of ours, who had taken service at Mongheer are dis-

August 13th.—The former news still prevails, which gives us great reason to think that it is true: we shall soon be out of doubts. Our friend had a servant from Boglepoor, which confirms the former news.

August 14th.—We have nothing new to-day, but additional circumstances of the former battle. Our servant in bringing in six bottles of wine was stopped by the fellow at the gate, and was not allowed to bring it in, and informs us we can't have any more without a fresh order from our new Governor.

August 15th.—No account of our army's advancing. We learn the Nabob has got to Boglepoor, and daily expect to hear something decisive. Our old friend has received a flying report that Ramnarain and Roybulab are both cut off; we hope it will prove without foundation.

August 16th.—The news of the two former being cut off prevails, with the additional circumstances that Messrs. Ellis and Lushington are also, likewise three *harcarras*, which makes us apprehensive that there is some truth in it, and that they have been found out in some correspondence.

charged the service, and ordered out of the province, lest they should save him as they did below.

Friday, August 19th.—By a servant arrived from Mongheer, Mr. Ellis, etc., are well, and Ramnarain, Raj bullab and his son were put in a boat, and it is believed were drowned. It is reported that the Nabob has made proposals of peace, and offered three crores of rupees to make good all damages, but this wants confirmation. His Excellency, for certain, has marched from Bauglepore.

Saturday, August 20th.—Heard by a messenger from His Excellency's camp that 500 Europeans, three battalions of sepoys, our own horse, had marched from Muxadabad towards Beerboom to the pass in the hills, while Meer Jaffier with his army, and 3 or 400 Europeons, and 5,000 black lately from Calcutta, with 1,600 sepoys remained behind. Both armies have artillery in proportion. It is said the Nabob has made a present of six months' pay to all his troops, is in possession of the passes, and ready for a run, not caring to leave Bauglepore.

Sunday, August 21st.—To-day Nobit Roy arrived to see his family, the Begum being at Jaffier Khan's garden. It is said they proceed up-country to a place in the hills near $\frac{\text{Muckeracous.}}{\text{Sasseram}}$

Monday, August 22nd.—Nothing extraordinary only some Armenians confined here.

Tuesday, August 23rd.—Fair and clear weather to-day, which gives us great joy, as the rain for these four days past has occasioned such a damp as affects our health, Mr. Campbell being sick.

Wednesday, August 24th.—Nothing extraordinary.

Thursday, August 25th.—By advices from Mongheer, hear his Excellency and the Armenian general are greatly in panic. Letters arrive here to the Begum twice a day, often in order to quicken her marches.

Friday, August 26th.—To-day the Begum set out on her march towards Rhotasgurrah. She has 1,500 bullock, 3 camels, 100 elephants, very many boats, besides elephant coaches; 1,200 horses, and 200 *burgundasses* are for the escort, having all his treasure with her, it is currently said, and, from some authority, His Excellency will follow in 15 or 20 days.

Saturday, August 27th.—Nothing extraordinary. Hear a Jamidar, from Buxier with 4,000 horse and foot, passed this place in his way down.

Sunday, August 28th.—Nothing extraordinary, only the Begum has halted at Puliaary.

Monday, August 29th.—Hear many Armenian and Portuguese are arrived here on account of the commotion below.

Tuesday, August 30th.—It is said our troops are yet at Sooti Nalla, that his Excellency has sent detachments down, that Gregan Cawn has no command, and a Jamedar who lately made his escape from Shujah Dowlat's country, where he was a prisoner, is appointed to the command in his stead. That His Excellency is still at Bauglepore. These three days past we can't get our allowance on account of the confusion here.

Wednesday, August 31st.—Yesterday evening had an account from the Padre that some troops have arrived and joined the army; they had divided, Meer Jaffier with part of his troops lay at a pass near Sooty; that a farcive battery on the side of a lake was raised by our troops under command of Major Carnac, while Major Adams of the 84th Regiment with Roydouleb has gone the Beerboon road. A party had secured the Purnea country, and stopped provisions from crossing. It is confirmed that all the best jamidars are gone down, that Gregan Cawn is degraded, because he promised an accommodation between His Excellency and his father-in-law. The Begum still continues her journey. We have a report that Dr. Fullerton has sent word to some of his black friends here that he will see them in a few days.

Thursday, September 1st.—To-day, heard some accounts of our gaining a complete victory at Sootyt Nulla, but not confirmed. This evening all the Armenian women set out to the westward.

Friday, September 2nd.—Nothing extraordinary.

Saturday, September 3rd.—Heard to-day, by a messenger from our camp at Sooty to a black merchant, that the armies remain there in their old position; that Major Adams had for certain gone the Beerboon road with a view to pass the hills; that yesterday an account of it had been sent here for them to keep a look-out, upon which many prepared for going off. The Seaths' houses here with his Gomastah's were seized and three lakhs of rupees. Nobit Roy with the Begum has arrived at Daudnagore. He has sent word to Ramnarain's family that he is not put to death, but in a secure place in Mongheer and in iron, with Raj bullab.

Sunday, September 4th.—Nothing extraordinary.

Monday, September 5th.—A report of our having possessed Maulda.

Tuesday, September 6th.—Hear'd to-day of some ships being arrived at Calcutta with seapoys, and Europeans. Boo Ali Cawn is returned to Baugle-pore, and Mindy Ally Cawn got command of the army below. Comdar Cawn is stopped in the hills, and can't pass. Things are said to be in the greatest confusion at His Excellency's quarters. This by letter.

Wednesday, September 7th.—By a messenger from Muxadabad in nine days, have the account of an action confirmed as follows: The enemy made an attack on our fascine battery at night. Our people quitted it, and having let about 4,000 men land (for they crosssd the nulla in boats), then immediately surrounded them and cut them off.

Thursday, September 8th.—Nothing extraordinary.

Friday, September 9th.—Saw a chit from Mr. Ellis to his writer, dated 3rd, wherein he tells him he should want him soon on his business at Patna, and therefore to remain there. It is said the Nabob has retreated 4 *coss*. There is some rumour of some troops coming up the other side of the river.

Saturday, September 10th.—We have from Nicolo some confused account of our storming the enemy's trench in the night, entirely driving them from thence, and taking all their camp and artillery. Somero and Marcott are missing, and the broken troops obliged to retreat. It is reported that six Jamidars who went with Comgar Cawn are gone off; things in the greatest confusion at His Excellency's court.

Sunday, September 11th.—We learn, by a packet from Chinsurah, that Messrs. Amyatt and Hay are ordered to Europe, Mr. Sumner is coming out second in Council, and Mr. McGuire buxey, so that Mr. Vansitart's interest seems to prevail, which may produce strange effects here. A messenger arrived from our camp who brings an account of the action which he says he heard from the Nabob's *harcarrahs*, that Mindy Ally Cawn and another Jamidar were killed, and all their guns and camp were taken, that a 20-gun ship and three sloops were coming up, and had passed Nadea Santipore.

Monday, September 12th.—Hear of six lakhs of rupees having arrived here from the Begum to pay the troops here.

Tuesday, September 13th.—Hear a rumour of our troops being in possession of the first pass, and that Mindy Ally Cawn is certainly killed; that Mr. Vansitart is suspended by the Council. A boy from Mongheer brings an account of Mr. Jones having arrived there in a *dooly*. Yesterday a Jamidar arrived at this place on some important business.

Wednesday, September 14th.—It is said the Jamidars have been ordered here to put the place in a posture of defence. The place is quite full of the defeat of His Excellency's troops, and the consequences of it. People are going off daily. He has retired himself to Mongheer, and it is

Fullarton.

September 13th.—Mr. Ellis and the rest of the gentlemen were sent from Mongheer; Messrs. Ellis and Guentree were in *palanquins;* Lushington, Smith, Lieutenant Bowen, Ensign McLeod, and one gentleman, whom I don't remember, were on horseback, the rest were in irons; some in *doolys*, and some in hacknies, and after their arrival at Patna, were confined in Hajee Ahmed's house.

affirmed we have a strong party coming through the hills, that all the passes are abandoned.

Thursday, September 15th.—Hear'd that the Armenian General is close prisoner, and a guard put over his effects here; also that the Jamidar commanding at Mongheer had refused admittance to His Excellency, and that our troops will be at this place as soon as his.

Friday, September 16th.—We have not these nine days had any allowance from the Nabob on account of the confusion here, the consequence of the late defeat of His Excellency's troops. Hear'd by a peon of Sir William Hope that Captain Turner died the night before $\frac{\text{he}}{\text{we}}$ left Mongheer. To-day we divided what cash remained in our possession which came to 30 rupees each, and have sent the greatest part of the effects of others who were with us to the Dutch factory. This precaution we have taken lest we be ordered to march up-country with His Ecellency.

Saturday, September 17th.—Received advices of our army for certain being at Shawbad, 3 *coss* above the upper pass, that His Excellency is destroying Mongheer and they are here destroying our factory-house and fortifying this place.

Sunday, September 18th.—His Excellency's people are going off in troops. Mirza Caliel and Mindy Ally Cawn are both arrived here, having fled from the late action. Our gentlemen are on their way from Mongheer to this place, and it is thought His Excellency intends pushing through the hills to Bengal, in order to draw our troops down, prolong time, and gain some assistance, which he may be in expectation of from above. To-day sent my superfluous clothes to the Dutch factory. We also received nine days' allowance out of eleven days due to us. Our peons here seem in great agitation and, in short, the whole city seems ready to take wing. Hear His Excellency is 3 *coss* this side of Mongheer, and our troops 16 *coss* from there.

Monday, September 19th.—To-day all our gentlemen, except Mr. Fullarton, arrived from Mongheer. It is said Lady Hope and some other women are left behind, most of the gentlemen are in irons. Captain Turner died of a fever at Mongheer. Our servant, Nicolo, in attempting to get in to the gentlemen, was made a prisoner, on account of his being dressed with a cross, sword, and target. No account of either our army or His Excellency's.

Tuesday, 20th, and Wednesday, 21st.—Nothing extraordinary: our servant, Nicolo, is released by making application at the Durbar. Hear the Dutch Chief has sent wine, etc., to Mr. Ellis.

Thursday, September 22nd.—Considerable rain with a great wind; it being the full moon and just at the equinox.

Friday, September 23rd.—As His Excellency still continues at Mongheer, it gives us reason to think our troops are not yet in possession of the upper pass.

Saturday, September 24th.—Nothing extraordinary. Hear for certain that our troops are at Shawbad, that the enemy are repairing what of Mongheer they had destroyed, that everything was in the greatest confusion in His Excellency's camp, that Somero had the management of everything. His Excellency had not eaten for three days, nor allowed his *nagar* to beat, that he and Somero were at Mongheer, and his army advanced to Gulgot Nulla, so that we may hourly expect some news.

Sunday, September 25th.—Nothing extraordinary.

Monday, September 26th.—This evening heard that ten Europeans at Bar had been tried and thrown into the river, so that from this we may guess what we are to expect. Also an account that some *perwannahs* have arrived here to several Jamidars, and that it is thought many are sent to Jamidars of His Excellency's camp. Some think that he will be laid hold of by his own people.

Fullarton

September 19th.—I was sent from Mongheer to Patna, and confined alone in the kila.

Tuesday, September 27th.—This morning hear that Lady Hope has arrived at the Dutch factory. A rumour prevails of His Excellency having been completely defeated a few days ago and lost every gun, etc., and that he is now on his way to Patna. The very peons are in great agitation on this account.

Wednesday, September 28th.—Heard from good authority that His Excellency is retreating, and was two days ago at Saidpur, Somero, and the Armenians with a party at Mongheer, and our army at Bauglepore. Also a party had crossed the river, and are coming up on the other side. Boo Ally Cawn with the Seaths, and several other persons were at Bar. Many prisoners have been released, amongst the rest Shaik Mahomed was released from this place, and put under the care of a friend of his in His Excellency's army, and goes out here to-morrow morning.

Thursday, September 29th.—Hear that His Excellency is 2 *coss* this side of Ruinalla and Somero with the Armenians at the Nulla, that his people are going off daily, and he is in great fear of his life. That about three weeks ago, he proposed cutting us all off, but was prevented by Somero, the Armenians and some of his Jamidars. The Moolidar with a good force will be at Hadgepore in three days, that His Excellency is striking off for the hills at Ramnasera within 8 *coss* of this place. It is believed that his orders would not be obeyed here, as most of the city seem willing to protect us. Gregan Cawn had 15 horses, which arrived here yesterday, but the gates were shut, and they were not permitted to enter. As things grow towards [a crisis, our situation must create as] much anxiety. It is said he will be at Ramnasera the day after to-morrow, so that our fate must be determined in two or three days at the farthest.

Saturday, October 1st.—Mahomet Emy Cawn with the Seaths and some other prisoners still remain without the east gate. 12 Europeans who came with him arrived in the city to-day.

Sunday, October 2nd.—Heard that His Excellency would be at Bar to-day, and our troops at

Ruinalla, that Gregan Cawn is either killed or badly wounded by his Moguls in a dispute about pay. Ten Europeans arrived here to-day.

Monday, October 3rd.—Hear that the Seaths and Mohamed Cawn are safely lodged in the city, and that the Jamedar sent his chobdar to Mr. Ellis yesterday, telling him not to be uneasy, and if he wanted money he would let him have it. Many of our guards have left us. Rice had risen within these few days to 6 seers for a rupee. Heard this night that His Excellency is at Bisionpore, and will pass this place to-morrow. Are told not to be uneasy, for we should be safe.

Tuesday, October 4th.—To-day. His Excellency arrived at Ramnarain's gardens, and to-morrow comes into the city. They have been very busy to-day, mounting guns on the bastion of this place. Heard that Meer Jaffier's brother had made his escape.

Wednesday, October 5th.—Heard the Seaths were cut off near Bar.

Thursday, October 6th.—Heard this morning that Mr. Ellis and 47 gentlemen were cut off last night, so that doubtless our fate must be in 24 hours, for which God prepare us all!

Fullarton.

October 5th.—Mr. Ellis with the rest of the gentlemen were inhumanly butchered by Somru, who came that evening to the place with two companies of sepoys (he had the day before sent for all the knives and forks from the gentlemen); he surrounded the house with his people and went into a little outer square, and sent for Messrs. Ellis, Hay, and Lushington, and with them came six other gentlemen, who were all terribly mangled, and cut to pieces, and their bodies thrown into a well in the square and it filled up; then the sepoys were sent into the large square, and fired on the gentlemen there, and rushing upon them cut them into pieces in the most inhuman manner, and they were thrown into another well, which was likewise filled up.

Friday, October 7th.—The Nabob sent for me, and told me to get myself in readiness to go to Calcutta, for that he had been unlucky in the war, which, he asserted with great warmth, had not been of his seeking, nor had he been the aggressor, reproaching the English with want of fidelity and breach of treaty, but he said he still had hopes of an accommodation; he asked me what I thought of it: I told him I made no doubt of it. When some of his people then present mentioned the affair of Mr. Amyatt's death, he declered that he had never given any orders for killing Mr. Amyatt, but after receiving the advice of Mr. Ellis having attacked Patna, he had ordered all his servants to take and imprison all the English in the provinces wherever they could find them; he likewise added that if a treaty was not set afoot, he would bring the King, the Marratoes, and Abdulla against us, and so ruin our trade, etc. He had finished his letters, and ordered boats and a guard to conduct me, when upon the advice of some of his people, he stopped me, and said there was no occasion for me to go. After sending for me at first, he ordered the sepoys, in whose charge I was, to go to their quarters; two Moguls and 12 *harearrahs* to attend me, but to let me go about the city where I pleased. I then applied for to have liberty to stay at the Dutch Factory which was granted. I applied to Mindialy Cawn for his interest on behalf of the gentlemen in the Chaalsatun who, where seven in number, and was not killed till the 11th of October; but when he was petitioned about them, he gave no answer, but sent orders to Sumro to cut them off. I likewise applied to Ally Ibrahim Cawn to intercede for them, but he gave no answer, either, though I was present when Ibrahim Cawn petitioned for them.

October 14th.—On the approach of our army, Cossim Ally decamped with his troops in great confusion and marched as far as Phulwari, five *coss* to the westward of the city. The *harcarrahs* that were with me having no orders about me, I gave them some money which made them pretty easy.

October 15th.—After giving money to a Jamidar that had the guard to the westward of the Dutch Factory by the riverside, I set out in a small *pulwar* and got rope to the boats under command of Captain Wedderburn, that were lying opposite to the city on the other side of the river and at 11 o'clock that night arrived at the army under the command of Major Adams, laying at Jutly.

List of Persons who suffered in the Massacre at Patna and at other places during the troubles.

Covenanted Servants.

Mr. Woolaston
" Amyatt } Killed at Muxadabad.

" Ellis
" Hay
" Chambers
" Lushington
" Howitt
" Lyon
" Oakes
" Smith
" Amphlett
" Bennett
" Gulston
" Egton
" Lake
" Hutchinson
" Round
" Collings
" Croke } Killed in the Massacre at Patna.

Military.

Captain Carstairs... Died of his wounds at the battle near Patna.

" Joecher
" Tabby
" Kinch } Killed in the Massacre at Patna.

Captain Turner ... Died of a flux at Mongheer.
" Wilson ... Killed in the Massacre at Patna.
" Parry ... Killed in the Assault at Patna.
" Summers Killed in the Massacre at Patna.
Lieutenant Hope... Ditto. ditto.
" Macdowall Killed in the Assault at Patna.
" Downie ... Ditto. ditto.

" Perry
" Roach
" Holland } Killed in the Massacre at Patna.

" Pickering Killed in the Battle near Chupra.
" Jones ... Killed in the Massacre at Patna.
" Cooper ... Killed at Muxdabad.

" Gordon
" Spunned
" Steuart } Killed in the Massacre at Patna.

Ensign Krafft ... Killed in the Battle at Chupra

" Blewitt, Senior
" Armstrong
" McKie
" Greentier
" McLeod
" Crawford
" Blewitt, Junior } Killed in the Massacre at Patna.

Lieut. Fireworker-Hamilton
" Parry } Killed in the Massacre at Patna.
" Bowen
" Reed } Killed in the Assault of Patna.

Surgeons.

Mr. Crook
" Anderson } Killed in the Massacre at Patna.
" Hans ... Died at Mongheer.

Private Merchants.

Mr. Campbell
" Harris
" Johnstone
" Plaice
" Folliott
" West
" Hewitt
" Allright
" Harling } Killed in the Massacre at Patna.
" Andrews
" Burslem } Killed at Rungpore.

Covenanted Servants	...	19
Military	... ...	32
Surgeons	... ...	3
Private Merchants...	...	11
		65

Of which were killed in the massacre at Patna 51.

APPENDIX I.

THE FOUR SERJEANTS.

Doctor Fullarton, who had some friends at court, had his life spared; and four British serjeants escaped.

These men were selected from the other prisoners, and sent to the Nabob of Purnea (as he was then called) and placed under his charge.

When Cossim Ally had determiued upon the destruction of the prisoners, he sent orders to Purnea for these men to be put to death. The Nabob, who happened to be a humane, good man, and being highly pleased with the conduct of the serjeants whilst with him, declined putting the orders in executiont He, however, wrote to Cossim Ally, entreating that he would recall his mandate, because he feared, if he was still determined upon it, it would be a difficult matter (as the men were beloved by all his people) to find one that would undertake the task. Cossim Ally, on the receipt of the letter, flew into a violent rage, and directed another order to be sent to the Nabob, in which he told him, that if he had not spirit himself to put his commands in force against those faithless and treacherous Englishmen, to send them immediately to Patna, where ample justice should be done, for the crimes they had committed.

On this letter being delivered to the Nabob, he sent for the serjeants and with tears in his eyes, informed them of the severe order he had received, and of the steps he had taken to preserve their lives; that he must now send them to Patna, where he hoped by the time they got there, the rage of Cossim Ally might be cooled, and that they might probably escape death. They were accordingly embarked on a Pattella boat, in charge of a jemadar and twelve burkendosses, and dropped down a small stream called the old, or little Cossy, which falls into the Ganges a little below Bissunpore Gola, and nearly opposite to Sickra Gully.

Here the serjeants had determined to have a chance for their lives. As soon as the boat had reached the Ganges, and hoisted sails for Patna, it being the height of the rains, two of them went up on the chopper, or roof, and saw the jemadar and three or four of his men asleep, with their faces covered. This they thought a favourable opportunity. They gently seized two of their swords which were near them, drew them from the scabbards, and having at the same time secured the matchlocks, one of them ran up to the manjee (helmsman) seized him by the arm, and threw him overboard: they then gave a hurra, which was the signal for the two below; who, in the meantime, were not idle. The noise waked those upon deck, who seeing the serjeants with drawn swords, fell upon their knees, and begged their lives, which were granted, provided no further resistance was made. The jemadar instantly called to his men below to surrender, which they did; so that the serjeants were in possession of the boat in less than ten minutes from their first going upon deck. The manjee having caught hold of the rudder, entreated to be taken on board, and promised that he would conduct them down the river. His request was complied with, and the moment he was placed in his former situation, the sails were hauled down, the boat put about, and the crew taking the oars, the gallant fellows had the good fortune, by sunset, to meet the British army under Major Adams, then advanced to Udda Nulla.

As all these deserving men have long since paid the debt of nature, the writer entreats he may be excused in giving a short account of them. Their names were Davis, Douglas, Speedy, and another whose name he cannot now recollect. Davis was a smart young man, and a native of Edinburgh. He enlisted in the Company's service in the year 1761 and was posted to Captain Sommors's company, one of those left at Patna, in which he was soon made a serjeant. After his escape from Purnea, he was put into the grenadiers, with which he served the whole war. Being posted to the 1st Brigade, that division of the army proceeded to Monghyr, where, in the year 1766, the general resignation took place. In this situation of things, Sir Robert Fletcher, who commanded the brigade, sent for Davis and offered him a commission; but he nobly refused it, declaring "that as the officers could not live upon their pay, which was the cause of their quitting the service, it was impossible he could." He was, however, the next year appointed Quartermaster to the three battalions sent to the coast under Lieutenant-Colonel William Smith, and on the return of that detachment in the year 1770, procured an ensign's commission, and died a captain in February, 1788.

Douglas was a brave soldier, and was long in the service of the Honourable Company in Bengal. On his joining the army at Udda Nulla, he was placed in the European Battalion, with which he served until the year 1766, when he was appointed serjeant-major to one of the Purgunnah battalions, then formed for the Revenue duty at Moradbaug.

Here he remained until the beginning of the year 1773, when the Sanassies becoming very troublesome in the district of Rungpore, Captain Timothy Edwards, who then commanded the battalion, was ordered out with five companies, to clear the province of those marauders. Having received his instructions from the Chief of Rungpore, he marched in quest of them, and the morning after, having crossed one of those small rivers with which the northern districts abound, he described the Sanassies about two miles in front of him. He immediately formed his detachment into a column by subdivisions from the right, and marched on towards the enemy, who, as soon as he came near enough, saluted him with a few rockets. When Captain Edwards thought himself within a proper distance for engaging he rode to the head of the column, and beat to arms, intonding that the divisions should double upon the left of the leading division as they came up; but the men mistaking the orders, wheeled to the left, and formed in battalion, which laid their right flank open to the enemy. Seeing the error they had fallen into he galloped to the left, in order to draw them into line, fronting the Sanassies, whilst Douglas exerted himself on the right for the same purpose; but it was too late, for the enemy, perceiving the confusion, rushed in upon them with their swords and spears and having dispatched a few put the rest to flight.

Douglas was one of the first that fell; but the fate of Captain Edwards was not known; hi hat was found in the Nulla before-mentioned, but the body has never been discovered.

The Native Commandant and Adjutant were tried for their misconduct in that unfortunate action, and were executed at the mouth of a cannon: but the gallant behaviour of one of the jemadars deserves much praise for having rallied sixteen men, he made his retreat good, although attacked on every side by the Sanassies; for which he was promoted to the rank of Subadar.

This was the third detachment which had been cut off by those religious plunderers; one commanded by a Captain Thomas, the other by Lieutenant Keith, who both lost their lives upon the occasion. As these parties were all from the Purgunnah battalions, it occasioned the dissolution of that establishment.

Serjeant Speedy, from whom the writer had the account of Captain Carstairs' detachment, was a steady soldier, and a man of long service in the field. He was a native of Ireland, and in the beginning of what is called the Spanish or ten years war, enlisted in the 32nd regiment of foot, then commanded by Colonel Huske. He accompanied his regiment to Flanders in the year 1742, and remained with it the whole war; was present at the battles of Dettingen, Fontenay, and Lafeldt; in the latter of which he lost two fingers of his left hand. The following year being 1748 he received his discharge, and immediately after enlisted in the Honourable East India Company's service. He arrived at Madras in 1749, and being posted to the grenadier company, was ordered to take the field under Major Lawrence, where he served the whole of the war against the French, in which many gallant actions were performed by the company he belonged to. In 1756 his Company composed part of the detachment sent round to Bengal, under Major Kilpatrick. And here the writer begs leave to observe, that the Company above-mentioned was the oundation of the grenadier company of the only European regiment belonging to our Honorable employers now in Bengal, and it affords him the highest gratification to learn, that on a late occasion, the officers and men composing it, nobly supported the character which it had acquired by their gallant predecessors fifty years before.

From the time of this arrival in Bengal, until he was posted to Captain Turner's battalion, in the year 1760, he was present in every action which occurred during that period. On his return from Purnea, he was posted to the European regiment in which he died in the year 1767.

The other serjeant was a man of great merit for his situation in life. Shortly after he joined the army from Purnea, he was appointed Serjeant-Major to Captain Scotland's battalion, then ordered to be raised at Midnapore, where he died in 1766.

(From Captain John William's *Historical Account of the Rise and Progress of the Bengal Native Infantry, 1817.*)

APPENDIX II.

Monghyr Fort taken.

[PROCEEDINGS, OCTOBER 17.]

From MAJOR ADAMS, *to the President.*

DEAR SIR,—I have the pleasure to acquaint you that we are now in possession of Monghyr, the breach being last night practicable, I intended to have stormed the fort this morning, but the enemy prevented us that trouble by surrendering at discretion. I believe there are near 300 pieces of cannon, 7 or 8 of them 24-pounders, all the rest Europe guns, about 1,000 stand of firelocks and a great quantity of matchlocks, with a large quantity of all sorts of ammunition and grain.

The massacre of the English at Patna.

[PROCEEDINGS, OCTOBER 26.]

We yesterday received the following letter from Major Adams, dated 18th instant :—

GENTLEMEN,—The accounts which I have communicated to the President relative to the fate of our Gentlemen at Patna are now confirmed by the arrival of several of their servants in Camp. One Assuck, consumah to Mr. Albright, who gives the most distinct account, I intend to send down to Calcutta for your examination. He says that 12 days ago, at 7 o'clock in the evening, our Gentlemen having drank Tea, were acquainted by Mr. Ellis' servant, that Someroo was arrived with some Sepoys, on which Mr. Ellis immediately ordered a chair to be brought for him, but instead of going to the Gentlemen, he sent away the Mogul who had the charge of them, and went into the back room and gave orders to the servants who were getting supper ready to be gone. He then sent for Messrs. Ellis and Lushington who being acquainted he had private business with them, immediately went to him and were instantly cut down ; afterwards Messrs. Hay, Lyon and Jones were sent for and despatched in the same manner, as were likewise Messrs. Chambers, Amphelett and Gulston who were next sent for with Mr. Smith, but he receiving a cut on the shoulder escaped into the room, and acquainted the rest of the Gentlemen who defended themselves with bottles and plates (their knives and forks being taken from them after dinner) and obliged the Sepoys to retire, who immediately loaded their pieces and shot them, 25 were in Irons, the abovementioned gentlemen with others amounting to 24 more were not in irons. He adds that Captain Wilson, Ensign Mackay, Doctor Campbell and five or six others were murdered at Chalisatoon, where they were confined, with Doctor Fullarton, who was the only gentleman that was not put to death. But that all the English soldiers were yet alive. This horrid massacre was perpetrated the night that Cossim Ally Khan received the President's and my letters.

All accounts likewise agree that Futta Sing, Ramnarain's brother, with 8 or 9 more of Ramnarain's relations were about the same time put to death, and that the Seats were put to death near Baur and their bodies not permitted to be burnt, but exposed under a Guard of Sepoys ; the bodies of our Gentlemen were most of them thrown into a well in the compound of the house they were confined in.

They likewise say that immediately on receipt of the news of our storming Ouda Nulla, Cossim Ally Khan ordered all the English to be sent out on the river and sunk there, but was prevented by Coja Gregory who, had he lived, they say, would have prevented this horrid affair.

I am, Gentlemen,
Your most obedient humble Servant

CAMP AT BURRIE,
18th October 1763. } THOS. ADAMS.

The Board's Resolution regarding the Massacre.

After reflecting with the most unfeigned sorrow and regret on this act of unparallelled and barbarous cruelty, which we have now no room left to doubt has been perpetrated at Patna by the emissaries of Cossim Ally Khan on the lives of our countrymen who were prisoners in his hands ; although in the ordinary and usual calamities of war it becomes the business of the Heads of a Government to avoid shewing any marks of public concern which may be attended with the bad effects of depressing the spirits of a Colony, yet as the situation of our affairs is such as to give no occasion for apprehending any ill consequences to our public operations from a contrary conduct at this time, and the present calamity being in itself of so singular and heavy a nature, we think it highly proper to enter upon some public methods of manifesting to the world our concern on this occasion, as well because it is a necessary tribute to the memory of the unfortunate gentlemen who have thus fallen the victims of a horrid cruelty, as that it will serve to testify to the Natives of the country the sentiments we feel for the loss of our friends and imply our resolution of revenging their untimely fate.

It is therefore agreed and ordered that a general deep mourning shall be observed in the settlement for he space of fourteen days to commence next Wednesday, the 2nd of November.

That the morning of that day shall be set apart and observed as a public fast and humiliation, and that intimation be accordingly given to the chaplains to be prepared with a sermon and forms of prayer suitable to the occasion.

That the evening before, immediately after firing the 8 o'clock gun, Minute guns shall be fired from the ships and the Fort which Commodore Tinker having been so obliging as to join us in the marks of our concern will begin from His Majesty's ship *Liverpool*, to be taken up first from the old, and next from the new Fort, and then to be succeeded by the *Osterley* and *Boscawen*, the Company's ships, which lay at anchor off town, and as Captain Tinker also mentions that he will send orders to the same effect to His Majesty's ships *Medway* and *York* at Kedgeree, that the Company's ships *Deptford*, *Lord Clive*, and *Pigot* which are laying at Culpee be directed to follow their example.

The better to answer the end proposed by adding to the solemnity of this ceremony, it is strictly ordered that the old Fort do not begin to fire till the *Liverpool* has ceased firing, the new Fort to take up the fire from the old Fort in the same manner, and so the ships according to the order they are here mentioned in.

After paying this necessary duty to the memory of our countrymen, we are futher agreed and determined to use all the means in our power for taking an ample revenge on the persons who may have been concerned in this horrid execution, and with a view of deterring in future all ranks and degrees of people from ordering or executing such acts of barbarity.

Resolved therefore that a Manifesto of the action be published throughout all the country, with a proclamation promising an immediate reward of a Lack of Rupees to any person or persons who shall seize and deliver up to us Cassim Ally Khan, and that he or they shall further receive such other marks of favour and encouragement as may be in our power to shew in return for this act of public justice.

That an immediate reward of Rs. 40,000 shall be given to any person or persons who shall apprehend the Chief named Summereau and bring him a prisoner to us.

APPENDIX III.

Page 1. *The Factory.*—Mr. Beveridge supposes this to be the present Opium Factory, but in 1767 we read that the English Factory was "entirely consumed" in the great fire. See Long. *Selections*, p. 479. It was on the river's edge to the west of the city walls. The hospital was inside the city.

Mutni bastion.—Mr. Beveridge notes: "This was one of the earthen mounds round Patna and was situated to the east of the Opium Factory. It was demolished at the time of the Mutiny." For the story of these mounds see *Calcutta Review*, Vol. LXXII., p. 205.

Marcar.—"An Armenian General of Gurghin-qhan's recommendation." *Seir Mutaqherin*, Vol. II., p. 451. The Armenians at this time seem to have martial inclinations and abilities. Gregore, another Armenian, was an important General of Mir Kassim's.

Page 2. *Large house near the killa called Chahalsatun.*—Here Azim-us-shan, Arangzeb's grand son, had resided. In an article on the "City of Patna," Mr. Beveridge writes: "The Chahal Satun, or forty-pillared residence of the Viceroys, stood just behind the mosque of the Madrasa. No trace of it now remains, and the site is a noisome jungle. Even in Buchanan's time it had quite disappeared, though fifty years before it had been the residence of Prince Ali Ghous, who was afterwards the Emperor Shah Allum. It was the failure of Carstairs to capture the citadel and the Chahalsatun that led to the disaster. See *Seiri Mutaqherin*, Vol. II., p. 473.

Philagi Pass.—Identified by Mr. Beveridge with Phalaza Ghat, near Deega.

Page 5. *Singia River.*—Singia was the site of the English Factory in Charnock's Patna period.

Meer Abdula.—A descendent of the Sufi Kings of Persia. "He was a friend of the English and was suspected by Mir Kasim. He had his house in Nozzerkattra close to the city wall. His father was Mir Gholam Ali. Nawab Wilayat Ali married a descendent of his." (Beveridge.)

Mirza Caleil (*Mirza Khalil*)—A merchant resident in Marufganj.

Page 6. (10th July.) *Our army being at Cutwa.*—Cutwa, a fortress, taken by Clive an his way to Plassey in 1757. As a matter of fact Cutwa was taken by Lieutenant Glenn on 17th July. See Broome, p. 372. An heavy engagement between Adams' forces and those under Taqui Khan took place on 19th July the English after their success resting at Plassey.

Page 10 (11th August) *An action below.*—Adams' victory at Gheria on 2nd August.

(24th September. *Nagar*=A small ceremonial drum.

Page 13. (27th September) Lady Hope, the wife of Sir William Hope, Bart., who perished in the massacre, afterwards married Wm. Lambert. See *Bengal : Past and Present*, Vol. ii. Part ii. p. 509.

The Dutch Factory.—(27th September. Mr. O'Malley writes: "The opium factory is said to occupy the site and contain some of the building, of the old Dutch factory. A large two storied building, which is now used as a godown, is pointed out as having been erected by the Dutch, and part of the revetment or river wall in the city is known as the Ollandaz Pushta, *i.e.*, the Dutch revetment." *Bengal District Gazettees*, *Patna*, p. 213. The Factory was seized by the English in 1781: restored to the Dutch in 1784, and finally ceded to the English by the treaty of 1784.

Page 14. (4th October.) *Abdulla against us.*—Ahmad Shah Abdali, the sovereign of the Afghans.